Past Masters

General Editor   Keith Thom

Russell

A. C. Grayling is Lecturer in Philosophy at Birkbeck College, London, and Senior Research Fellow at St Anne's College, Oxford. The author of *An Introduction to Philosophical Logic*, *The Refutation of Scepticism*, and *Berkeley: The Central Arguments*, he has also written *Wittgenstein* for the Past Masters series and edited *Philosophy: A Guide Through the Subject*.

Past Masters

Forthcoming

A. C. Grayling

Russell

Oxford   New York

OXFORD UNIVERSITY PRESS

Oxford University Press, Great Clarendon Street, Oxford OX2 6DP

Oxford New York
Athens Auckland Bangkok Bogota Bombay
Buenos Aires Calcutta Cape Town Dar es Salaam
Delhi Florence Hong Kong Istanbul Karachi
Kuala Lumpur Madras Madrid Melbourne
Mexico City Nairobi Paris Singapore
Taipei Tokyo Toronto
and associated companies in
Berlin Ibadan

Oxford is a trade mark of Oxford University Press

British Library Cataloguing in Publication Data
Data available

Library of Congress Cataloging in Publication Data
Data available
ISBN 0–19–287683–X

10 9 8 7 6 5 4 3 2

Printed in Great Britain by
Biddles Ltd., Guildford and King's Lynn

Preface

RUSSELL lived long and did much. He is one of the relatively small number of philosophers whose names are popularly known, and who in their life and work have come to seem emblematic of the great tradition of thought they represent. The reputation Russell enjoyed among his contemporaries rested on the multiplicity of contributions he made—often highly controversial ones—to social, moral, political, and educational debates. But his claim to an enduring fame rests on his outstanding technical contributions to logic and philosophy. In what follows I survey his life's work in both spheres. The aim throughout is to give as clear an account of them as brevity allows. Because this is not the place for detailed evaluation of philosophical arguments, still less of technicalities in mathematical logic, I give most houseroom to exposition; but I venture some discussion also, the themes of which can be pursued by consulting the literature cited in the Further Reading section, which shows the way for anyone who, having paddled in the surf here, might like to go for the swim. However, readers not especially interested in the more technical reaches of logic and philosophy can forgo Chapters 2 and 3, and can concentrate instead on the story of Russell's life and his contributions to public debate, as told in Chapters 1 and 4.

I am grateful to Keith Thomas and the Press's keen-eyed reader for comments, to Ken Blackwell for prompt help and documents from the Russell Archive, and to Alex Orenstein and Ray Monk for related and relevant discussion. My thanks go also to Leena Mukhey for her work on the index.

This is dedicated to Sue—'*dulces dominae Musa Licymniae cantus, me voluit dicere*'.

A.C.G.

London
1996

Contents

Note on References

RUSSELL wrote much, and his work has been reprinted often and in a variety of editions, the paginations of which do not always agree. Here are the principal works cited in the text in the editions consulted, with the abbreviations employed for those most frequently occurring.

A   *The Autobiography of Bertrand Russell* (London: Unwin Paperbacks, One Volume edn., 1975).

AMd   *The Analysis of Mind* (London: Allen & Unwin, 1921).

AMt   *The Analysis of Matter* (London: Routledge, paperback edn., 1992).

HK   *Human Knowledge: Its Scope and Limits* (London: Allen & Unwin, 1948).

HSEP *Human Society in Ethics and Politics* (London: Allen & Unwin, 1954).

PLA   'The Philosophy of Logical Atomism', in Marsh (ed.), *Logic and Knowledge*.

MM   *Marriage and Morals* (London: Routledge, paperback edn., 1991).

MPD   *My Philosophical Development* (London: Routledge paperback edn., 1993).

OKEW *Our Knowledge of the External World* (London: Allen & Unwin, 2nd edn., 1926).

PM   *Principia Mathematica* (Cambridge: Cambridge University Press, 2nd edn., 1925).

PoM   *The Principles of Mathematics* (London: Allen & Unwin, 1937; first published 1903).

PP   *The Problems of Philosophy* (Oxford: Oxford University Press, 1912).

An Inquiry into Meaning and Truth (London: Allen & Unwin, 1940).

The Conquest of Happiness (London: Allen & Unwin, 1930).

Education and the Social Order (London: Allen & Unwin, 1931).

Essays in Analysis, ed. Douglas Lackey (London: Allen & Unwin, 1973).

Introduction to Mathematical Philosophy (London: Allen & Unwin, 1919).

Logic and Knowledge, ed. R. C. Marsh (London: Allen & Unwin, 1956).

Mysticism and Logic (London: Allen & Unwin, paperback edn., 1963).

Power (London: Allen & Unwin, 1938).

Principles of Social Reconstruction (London: Allen & Unwin, 1916).
Religion and Science (Oxford: Oxford University Press, 1935).
Why I Am Not A Christian (London: Allen & Unwin, 1957).
Political Ideals (London: Routledge, 1994; first published 1917).
Roads to Freedom (London: Allen & Unwin, 1918).
Portraits from Memory (London: Allen & Unwin, 1958).

1 Life and Work

Russell is one of the best-known philosophers of the twentieth century. His fame—at times, his notoriety—was chiefly the product of his engagement in social and political controversy. He was a familiar public figure for nearly sixty years, featuring in the popular press sometimes as a subject of scandal and sometimes, in his respectable periods, as a pundit; in which role he also appeared as a broadcaster. He had much to say about war and peace, morality, sexuality, education, and human happiness. He published many popular books and articles, his views earning him a wide range of responses, from prison sentences to a Nobel Prize.

But his greatest contributions, and the true basis of his reputation, lie in the technical fields of logic and philosophy. So pervasive is his influence both on the matter and style of twentieth-century English-speaking philosophy that he is practically its wallpaper. Philosophers use techniques and ideas developed from his work without feeling the need—sometimes without recognizing the need—to mention his name; which is influence indeed. In this way he is a far more significant contributor to philosophy than his pupil Ludwig Wittgenstein. Philosophy learned some valuable lessons from Wittgenstein, but from Russell it acquired an entire framework, constituting what is now called 'analytic philosophy'.

In this label 'analysis' means rigorous examination of philosophically important concepts, and the language which embodies them, using methods and ideas derived from formal logic. Russell did not, of course, create analytic philosophy unaided. He was influenced by the logicians Giuseppe Peano and Gottlob Frege, and by his Cambridge colleagues G. E. Moore and A. N. Whitehead. Other influences were the seventeenth- and eighteenth-century thinkers René Descartes, Gottfried Leibniz, George Berkeley and David Hume. Indeed his first philosophical book was a sympathetic study of the second of these. But he brought these influences together in such a way that they offered a new approach to philosophical problems, illuminating them by a sharp new logical light.

By this means he played a central role in revolutionizing twentieth-century philosophy in the anglophone tradition.

Russell was accordingly a philosopher in both the popular sense, as a sage and teacher of mankind, and in the professional academic sense. In the chapters that follow I describe his contribution in both these philosophical guises. In the present chapter I sketch his long, rich, and sometimes tumultuous life, which in its sum and variety constitutes one of the most heroic biographies of modern times.

Bertrand Arthur William Russell was born on 18 May 1872 into a famous family, a cadet branch of the Dukes of Bedford. His paternal grandfather was the celebrated Lord John Russell who introduced the Reform Bill of 1832, which was the first step towards democratization of Parliament. Lord John was twice Prime Minister—from 1846 to 1852 and from 1865 to 1866—and was raised to an earldom by Queen Victoria. Russell's maternal grandfather, Lord Stanley of Alderley, had been a political ally of Lord John.

Russell's parents were an unusual and controversial couple, committed to progressive causes such as family planning and votes for women. His father, Viscount Amberley, chose John Stuart Mill as his godfather in a non-religious sense. Mill died just before Russell's first birthday, so his influence, though considerable, was indirect.

Amberley was briefly a Member of Parliament, but his political career collapsed when it became publicly known that he supported the idea of contraception. An example of the Amberleys' advanced views is afforded by the case of D. A. Spalding, a clever young scientist employed as tutor to Russell's elder brother Frank. Spalding was severely consumptive, and therefore in no position to marry and have a family. The Amberleys decided that this was no reason for him to be celibate, so Russell's mother 'allowed him', as Russell puts it in his *Autobiography*, 'to live with her'—to which he adds, 'though I know of no evidence that she derived any pleasure from doing so' (*A* 12).

Russell's mother and sister died of diphtheria in 1874 when he was aged 2, and his father's death followed eighteen months later. Amberley had appointed two agnostics as guardians for his sons —Spalding was one of them—but their grandparents, Earl Russell and his wife, strenuously objected. They went to law to overturn Amberley's will, and took their grandsons to live with them at Pembroke Lodge, a Royal grace-and-favour house in Richmond Park. Frank, seven years' Russell's senior, found life there intolerable, and rebelled. He was sent away to school. Bertie, more tractable and sweet-tempered, was kept at home. His grandfather died a mere three years later, and he was then entirely under the influence of his strait-laced Scottish Presbyterian grandmother, a daughter of the second Earl of Minto. Russell's character has often been explained, even—when occasion seems to demand it— excused, by reference to his aristocratic origins; but its first moulding was more truly the work of his grandmother's puritanism, characteristic rather of middle- than upper-class Victorianism. In the flyleaf of the Bible she gave him for his twelfth birthday she inscribed one of her favourite texts: 'Thou shalt not follow a multitude to do evil.' This remained a principle for Russell throughout his life.

It was a lonely but not, to begin with, an unhappy childhood. Russell had German and Swiss governesses, and early spoke German as fluently as English. He conceived a love for the extensive grounds of Pembroke Lodge, with their handsome views of the surrounding country. 'I knew each corner of the garden,' he wrote, 'and looked year by year for the white primroses in one place, the redstart's nest in another, the blossom of the acacia emerging from a tangle of ivy' (*A* 26). But as adolescence encroached, his isolation, intellectual as well as emotional, grew increasingly painful. He was alone in a household of old people remote from him in every way. A succession of tutors was his only tenuous link with the larger world. Nevertheless he was saved from too great unhappiness by nature, books, and later, mathematics. One of his uncles had an interest in science, which he communicated to Russell, helping to spur his mental awakening. But the real epoch occurred when he was 11 years old and his brother began to teach him geometry. Russell said the experience was 'as dazzling as first love' (*A* 30). After he had mastered the fifth proposition as easily as its predecessors, Frank told him that people generally found it difficult—it is the famous *pons asinorum* which puts a stop to many a budding geometrical career. 'This was the first time', wrote Russell, 'that it had dawned upon me that I might have some intelligence.' But there was a fly in the ointment: Euclid begins with axioms, and when Russell demanded proof of them Frank replied that they just had to be accepted, otherwise geometry could not proceed. Russell reluctantly accepted this, but the doubt raised in him at that moment remained with him, determining the course of his subsequent work on the foundations of mathematics.

In 1888 Russell went as a boarder to an Army crammer to prepare for Cambridge University scholarship examinations. His time there was made unpleasant by what he viewed as coarse behaviour among some of the other youths. Nevertheless he won a scholarship to Trinity College and entered there in October 1890 to read mathematics.

He felt as if he had stepped into paradise. Alfred North Whitehead, with whom he later collaborated in writing *Principia Mathematica*, had examined his scholarship papers, and told a number of the more gifted undergraduates and dons to look out for him. He accordingly found himself in highly congenial company, no longer intellectually isolated, and with friendship, based upon a mutuality of interests and intelligence, at last open to him.

In his first three years Russell read mathematics. His fourth he devoted to philosophy, studying under Henry Sidgwick, James Ward, and G. F. Stout. The Hegelian philosopher J. M. E. McTaggart was at that time influential among Cambridge's students and younger dons. He led Russell to think of British empiricism—represented by Locke, Berkeley, Hume, and John Stuart Mill—as 'crude', and gave him a taste instead for Kant and especially Hegel. Under Stout's influence Russell became an admirer of the neo-Hegelian Oxford philosopher F. H. Bradley, and carefully studied his works, which promote a version of the philosophical view known as 'idealism'.

But it was a younger contemporary who most decisively influenced Russell. This was G. E. Moore, who like Russell began as a Hegelian but soon repudiated that philosophy, persuading Russell to follow. Bradley had argued that everything believed by common sense, such as plurality and change in the world of things, is mere appearance, and that reality is in truth a single mental Absolute. With a heady sense of liberation Moore and Russell rejected this view. Although they thereafter developed in different ways, and although Russell in particular struggled hard to find satisfactory alternatives, the philosophical work of both was squarely premissed on realism and pluralism (see p. 26 for an explanation of these terms).

But the Moore-led rebellion came later. Russell was awarded a First Class in the Mathematics Tripos in 1893, being placed seventh Wrangler, and a First Class with distinction in the Moral Science Tripos the following year ('moral science' used to be Cambridge's name for subjects such as philosophy and economics). He then began writing a Fellowship dissertation on the foundations of geometry, a Kantian exercise representative of his outlook at the time. During the course of these excitements he came of age, and was therefore free to do something he had been planning in the face of his family's strong disapproval, namely, to marry Alys Pearsall Smith, an American Quaker five years his senior. He had met and immediately fallen in love with her in 1889, although she had not reciprocated his sentiments until four years later. Russell's family thought her highly unsuitable, and told him that in any case he should not have children because there was insanity in his family—both his Uncle William, who was in an asylum for the insane, and his Aunt Agatha, who had experienced delusions and was growing increasingly eccentric with age, were cited as proof.

In an attempt to detach him from Alys, Russell's family arranged for him to serve as honorary attaché at the British Embassy in Paris. They no doubt hoped that the allurements of the Naughty Nineties' capital might satisfy whatever impulses were driving him to a matrimonial bed. But the puritan education imposed on him by his grandmother had been altogether too effective; it scuppered the plan, as shown by the letters—paradigms of priggishness—in which Russell wrote home complaining of Parisian life. 'In Paris everybody is wicked,' he wrote, 'and every time one looks around one sees some blasphemy against love—they make me quiver with disgust.' As soon as he was in control of his own finances (he had a comfortable patrimony of £600 a year, and his bride had money too) Russell married Alys, and to begin with they were happy.

Russell's dissertation earned him a fixed-term research Fellowship at Trinity with no duties attached, which meant that he had neither to teach nor to reside in Cambridge. Accordingly he and

Alys went to Berlin where Russell studied German social democracy and wrote a book about it. This was his first book—the
first in an extraordinary total of seventy-one books and booklets
(leaving aside countless articles) published during his lifetime.
While in Berlin he conceived the idea of undertaking a vast project
of research, in which two lines of enquiry, one into the natural
sciences and the other into social and political questions, would
eventually converge to form a 'grand encyclopaedic work'. Russell
was still then influenced by Hegelianism, of which such a project
is typical; but the plan survived his radical change of philosophical outlook, although it did not take so systematic a form,
for among his many works Russell indeed wrote much on both
theoretical and practical questions.

German Social Democracy was followed a year later by the
published form of his Fellowship dissertation, *An Essay on the
Foundations of Geometry*. Then in 1900 Russell published *A
Critical Exposition of the Philosophy of Leibniz*. It was an accident, but an important one for him, that he came to write this
book. A Cambridge colleague who usually lectured on Leibniz
asked Russell to stand in for him one year, and Russell, who had
not had an opportunity to study Leibniz in detail, welcomed the
challenge. The book grew out of his lectures. Although Russell
disagreed with the main tenets of Leibniz's philosophy, aspects
of it remained influential in his thought.

By the time he was giving his Leibniz lectures Russell had been
persuaded by Moore to abandon idealism. Shortly afterwards
his interest in the philosophy of mathematics—specifically, in
the question whether mathematics can be supplied with logical
foundations, and thus be rendered certain—was given powerful
impetus by his encounter with the Italian logician Giuseppe Peano
at the International Congress of Philosophy in Paris in July 1900.
Peano was responsible for certain technical developments in logic
which suggested to Russell ways of carrying out the desired re-
duction of mathematics to logic. He avidly read Peano's works,
then began to improve, extend, and apply the methods they contained. In the first flush of excitement, and in just a few months,
he wrote a complete draft of what was to prove his first major
treatise, *The Principles of Mathematics*. He worked on revisions
and improvements for another year, and the book was published

in 1903. In writing a Preface for a new edition in 1937 Russell said
that he remained convinced of the truth of the book's fundamental thesis, which is 'that mathematics and logic are identical'.

The intellectual intoxication felt by Russell in 1900 never thereafter returned. For one thing, events in his private life during the
following years brought dark clouds. He found that he had lost his
love for his wife, and told her so. 'I believed in those days (what
experience has taught me to think possibly open to doubt) that
in intimate relations one should speak the truth,' he later wrote
(*A* 151). The result was great misery for them both in the nine
further years during which they shared an address. At nearly the
same time a revolution was wrought in his emotional life by wit-
nessing the suffering in illness of Evelyn Whitehead, wife of his
former teacher Alfred North Whitehead. Seeing her in the intense
isolation endured by one in agony, his view of the world suddenly
changed; to that moment he subsequently dated his pacifism, his
longing for children, the beginnings of a heightened aesthetic
sensibility, and a profound sense that each of us is ultimately and
irremediably alone. The experience is movingly described in his
Autobiography.

In his mathematical work, which otherwise might have afforded
him consolation, there occurred a similarly grave upheaval. This
was the discovery of a contradiction at the very heart of the project
Russell was trying to carry out. The contradiction and its importance is described in its due place in Chapter 2 below. Its effect
was to stall Russell's work for over two years, during which he
stared at a blank sheet of paper wondering how to proceed. By this
time he was at work on *Principia Mathematica*, which began life
as an intended second volume to *The Principles of Mathematics*.
This putative second volume was to have contained the technical working-out of the ideas sketched in *The Principles*, together
with a fuller treatment of a number of difficulties left over from
it; but it quickly became apparent that much more was needed if
he was to achieve the project's aim, which was 'to show that all
pure mathematics follows from purely logical premisses and uses
only concepts definable in logical terms' (*MMD* 57). Russell therefore invited Whitehead's collaboration, and from then until 1910
most of his mental energies were devoted to the production of
this monumental work. Its philosophical aspects, and the actual

writing out of the technical material, fell to Russell; Whitehead, among other things, made significant contributions to the notation and a great deal of working out of proofs.

Russell reports that he worked at *Principia Mathematica* for eight months each year, and from ten to twelve hours a day. When the manuscript was at last delivered to Cambridge University Press it was so huge that it had to be transported there in a four-wheeler carriage. The Syndics of the Press calculated that the book would bring them a loss of £600, and said that they were willing to bear only half that sum. Russell and Whitehead persuaded the Royal Society to help by voting a £200 grant, but the remainder had to be supplied from their own pockets. As a result, their financial reward for years of work on this vast project was a loss of £50 each.

But the true rewards were great. In the course of the endeavour, and arising from it, Russell published some very important philosophical papers. He was elected a Fellow of the Royal Society at the unusually young age of 35. His place in the history of logic and philosophy was secured. Much that Russell later attempted and achieved in his many spheres of activity was made possible by his having earned the Olympian stature conferred by authorship of *Principia*.

Russell was not idle in other respects during these years of intellectual labour. His interest in politics remained lively; he campaigned for free trade, and stood as a parliamentary candidate on behalf of female suffrage at the Wimbledon by-election of 1907. Votes for women was an intensely unpopular cause whose champions regularly suffered abuse and even violence. Russell might eventually have entered Parliament had his agnosticism not stood in the way; he was about to stand as a candidate for Bedford in the 1911 election when his local campaign organizers learned that he would not conceal his agnosticism from the electors, and would not go to church. They accordingly chose another candidate.

But something much more congenial then offered: Trinity appointed him to a five-year lectureship, so Russell assumed the life of a don, and turned his attention to writing a little book that became a classic: *The Problems of Philosophy*, which remains to this day one of the best short introductions to the subject.

One unexpected result of Russell's political activities was romance. In 1910, while living near Oxford, he helped canvass for the local candidate Philip Morrell, whose wife Lady Ottoline Morrell he had known in childhood. Their re-encounter blossomed in the following year into a love affair. Russell wished to marry her, which would have meant his divorcing Alys and Ottoline's divorcing Philip. But Ottoline did not wish to leave Philip, so the affair remained adulterous, with the compliance of Philip but the bitter opposition of Alys and her family. Russell and Alys separated and did not meet again for forty years, although they were in the meantime divorced, early in the 1920s.

Ottoline was indisputably good for Russell. 'She laughed at me', Russell wrote, 'when I behaved like a don or a prig, and when I was dictatorial in conversation. She gradually cured me of the belief that I was seething with appalling wickedness which could only be kept under by iron self-control. She made me less self-centred and less self-righteous' (*A* 214). She also provided him, in her person and the voluptuous beauty of her surroundings, with satisfactions for his aesthetic impulses. Russell was then nearly 40 years of age; it was a late but profound awakening.

In 1914 Russell visited the United States and lectured, among other places, at Harvard University. His lectures were subsequently published as *Our Knowledge of the External World*. One of his pupils at Harvard was T. S. Eliot, who wrote a poem about him, 'Mr Apollinax', in which he appears as a mythical creature, strange and even frightening, whose seaweed-festooned head might suddenly roll under a chair or pop up, grinning, above a screen; who laughs, Eliot says, 'like an irresponsible foetus', yet whose 'dry and passionate talk' eats up the afternoon, reminding Eliot of the beating of a centaur's hoofs on hard ground. It was an encounter that left a strong impression on Eliot; of the others present he could remember only that they ate cucumber sandwiches.

While visiting Chicago Russell fell in love with his host's daughter—she is unnamed in his autobiography—who was then a student at Bryn Mawr. They made plans for her to join him in England so that they could marry when he divorced Alys. She did indeed come; but by then the First World War had begun, the emotional shock of which to Russell, and his passionate engagement in pacifist activities, had obliterated his feelings for her. The disaster of her visit was later compounded by her going mad. In his autobiography Russell reports this sad interlude with agonized regret.

Russell's response to the outbreak of war was complex. He was too old to be a combatant, so he never had the status of a conscientious objector. (A number of his acquaintances who were in this position, such as Lytton Strachey, discharged their compulsory agricultural duties by pottering about Ottoline's country estate at Garsington.) Like many Edwardian intellectuals Russell had a tenderness for Germany and German culture. He was fluent in the language, read German books as a matter of course, and had lived there and written about its politics. But he was also intensely patriotic, once writing that 'love of England is very nearly the strongest emotion that I possess'. Nor was he an unconditional pacifist, as shown by the fact that a quarter of a century later he strongly supported the war against Nazism. The point for him was that the outbreak of hostilities in 1914 served no principle and promised no benefits, but was brought about by the folly of politicians and threatened to engulf civilization in a huge welter of wasted young life. 'All this madness,' he wrote in a letter to the *Nation* very soon after fighting began, 'all this rage, all this flaming death of our civilisation and our hopes, has been brought about because a set of official gentlemen, living luxurious lives, mostly stupid, and all without imagination and heart, have chosen that it should occur rather than that any of them should suffer some infinitesimal rebuff to his country's pride.'

Then as in the Vietnam War half a century later Russell was extraordinarily insightful. The horrendous slaughter of the trenches had not properly begun, yet Russell saw its inevitability, and with it much longer-term evil consequences. Very few could then have foreseen that a process had begun which would trap most of the world in actual or incipient war for most of the rest of the century, with scores of millions of deaths and the misdirection of massive resources to development of military technology, each new advance in the sophistication of which has been more dangerous and destructive than the last. Russell could not of course in 1914 foresee Bolshevism, Nazism and the Holocaust, nuclear weapons and the Cold War, nationalism given teeth by the international arms trade, and fundamentalism spurred by the jealous gap between rich and poor nations. But he had a lively sense that the outbreak of war meant that a gate had been swung wide to disaster of some form: and many decades of disaster duly followed.

He was equally horrified by the popular support for war in the combatant nations, and the form it took of 'primitive barbarism' and the release of 'instincts of hatred and blood lust', which—as he pointed out—are the very things civilization exists to oppose. Worst of all was the appearance of these same sentiments in the majority of his friends and acquaintances. He could not stand aside; throughout the war years he wrote articles and made speeches, supporting organized opposition to the war in the form of the Union of Democratic Control and the No Conscription Fellowship. Early in the war he did charitable work among Germans living in England who had been made destitute by being cut off from home. The need for this work did not last long because citizens of enemy nations were soon interned.

The leader of the No Conscription Fellowship was a young man called Clifford Allen (later Lord Allen of Hurtwood), who was repeatedly sent to prison for refusing to give up his anti-war work. At one of Allen's trials Russell met Lady Constance Malleson, an actress with the stage-name of Colette O'Neil. She was engaged in pacifist work also, spending her evenings in the theatre and her days stuffing envelopes in the Fellowship's offices. They became lovers, her calmness providing Russell with a refuge from the harshness of the wartime struggle.

Russell was himself several times on the rough end of the law for his anti-war work. In 1916 he was prosecuted because of an article he had written, and was fined £100. He refused to pay, so his goods were distrained; but his friends kindly bought them and gave them back to him, rendering his gesture futile. Then he was banned from entering any militarily restricted areas of Britain, in particular any part of the coast (to prevent him, he wryly supposed, from signalling to enemy submarines). He was refused a passport when he attempted to travel to America in 1916. And in 1918 he was sent to prison for six months because of an article in which he said that American troops coming to Europe might be used for strike-breaking, a task they had performed in their own country. Because of his connections (it was, as he sardonically acknowledged, useful being an Earl's brother) he was placed in the first division, which meant that he had a cell to himself and could have books; so he read and wrote, producing one book—*An Introduction to Mathematical Philosophy*—and the beginnings of another—*The Analysis of Mind*—together with a number of reviews and articles. He was released in September 1918, when it was already apparent that the war could not last much longer.

The first of Russell's brushes with the law carried an extra penalty. All the younger dons at Trinity had gone off to fight, leaving a small group of older men in charge of the College's affairs. They were deeply hostile to Russell's war-work. When they heard of his conviction, they voted to deprive him of his lectureship. The mathematician G. H. Hardy, outraged by this treatment of Russell, later wrote an account of it. When at the war's end the younger dons returned from fighting, they voted to reinstate Russell, but by that time Russell's interests were leading him abroad.

Among the many changes effected in Russell by the war was a widening in the scope of his literary activity. He produced two non-philosophical books during these years, *Principles of Social Reconstruction* (in the United States called *Why Men Fight*), published in 1916, and *Roads to Freedom*, published in 1918, which presaged his many further popular books on social, political, and moral questions. While giving *Principles of Social Reconstruction* as a series of lectures in 1916 Russell met and began what was intended to be a collaboration with D. H. Lawrence, but Lawrence's attitude soon turned hostile. At first Lawrence's accusations that Russell's pacifism was a mask for violently misanthropic feelings troubled Russell profoundly, because he thought Lawrence had special insight into human nature; but Lawrence's increasingly hysterical and vituperative letters led Russell to see through Lawrence's proto-fascistic brand of politics and his worship of irrationalism, and relations between them ceased.

In prison in 1918 Russell worked, as noted, on two philosophical books. His return to philosophy had however begun earlier, for in the early months of 1918 he gave a series of lectures under the title 'The Philosophy of Logical Atomism', published shortly afterwards in successive numbers of a journal called *The Monist*. In his characteristically overgenerous way, Russell attributed his ideas to Ludwig Wittgenstein, who had been his pupil for a short time at Cambridge before the war. In fact most of the ideas in Russell's lectures are apparent in work he did long before meeting Wittgenstein; but as one can see from the latter's *Tractatus Logico-Philosophicus*, written while Wittgenstein was serving at the front in the Austrian army, the two had discussed these ideas at some length before the war. Now Russell received a letter from Wittgenstein, who was languishing in an Italian prisoner-of-war camp, telling him about the *Tractatus*. After the Italians released him Wittgenstein tried to get his book published, but failed; so Russell lent his help, and persuaded a publisher to take the book by agreeing to write an introduction to it. Although Russell was several more times of crucial help to Wittgenstein—not least in arranging a research fellowship for him at Trinity a decade later—the two men drifted apart because of profound temperamental and philosophical differences.

Russell had once again fallen in love, this time with a young Girton graduate called Dora Black. In 1920 they independently visited the Soviet Union, from which Dora returned enthusiastic and Russell hostile. He wrote a damning book about the Bolsheviks, over which he and Dora quarrelled. But it did not stop them going together to China in 1921, where Russell had been invited to spend a year as a visiting professor in Peking.

As with many who spend any length of time in China, Russell fell in love with it. And like many of these many, he was inclined to romanticize the Chinese themselves. He applauded their sense of humour, their sagacity, their enjoyment of beautiful things, and their immensely civilized love of culture and learning. But he somehow did not see how vilely harsh were the lives of the majority in that vast country, nor how crushed and obstructed China was by its ancient traditions. While there he refused to set himself up as an adviser to the many who asked him how they should live, what they should think, and how China could emerge from its poverty and feudal disarray. The American philosopher John Dewey was visiting China at the same time, and did not hesitate to pronounce on all these matters, with the result that his memory remains a more potent influence in China today than Russell's. The tradition of the sage is strong in China; Russell therefore lost an opportunity to do much good there. He wrote a book setting out his views on China and its future, but a book published later in far-away England was no substitute for the oracles his guests had hoped to hear. He lectured them, instead, on mathematical logic.

Towards the end of his sojourn in Peking Russell fell seriously ill with bronchitis, and nearly died. As a result of the overzeal-ousness of some Japanese journalists, news of his death was an-nounced; Russell was therefore able to read his own obituary notices, including a one-liner that appeared in a missionary journal and especially amused him: 'Missionaries may be par-doned', it read, 'for breathing a sigh of relief at the news of Mr Bertrand Russell's death.'

Alys had at last agreed to a divorce, so when Russell and Dora returned to England in September 1921 they married, and not long afterwards their first son, John Conrad, was born. A daughter, Kate, followed two years later. Russell twice stood for Parliament as a Labour Party candidate in Chelsea, in 1922 and 1923, but unsuccessfully. Family responsibilities pressed; he needed to make a living, and therefore again gave up the idea of parliamentary politics to devote himself to writing and lecturing. The most luc-rative lecturing circuit was the United States, to which he made four visits during the 1920s. The popular books he published in-cluded *The A.B.C. of Relativity*, *The A.B.C. of Atoms*, *What I Believe*, *On Education*, *Sceptical Essays*, *Marriage and Morals*, and *The Conquest of Happiness*. Some of these were financially successful, and some caused scandal, mainly because of their lib-eral views on sexual morality. Nor did he neglect philosophy; his *Analysis of Mind*, begun in prison, appeared in 1921; he was in-vited to give the Tarner Lectures in Cambridge in 1925, and they were published in 1927 as *The Analysis of Matter*. He also pro-duced an introductory textbook called *An Outline of Philosophy*.

The advent of children satisfied a long yearning in Russell. They provided him with a 'new emotional centre' which absorbed him in parental interests for the rest of the 1920s. He bought a house in Cornwall so that the family could spend their summers there, and when John and Kate reached school age he and Dora decided to found their own school so that the children would be educated as they thought best. They rented Russell's brother's country house on the South Downs, and began a school of twenty children all roughly of the same age. The house was large, set in two hundred acres of virgin forest filled with magnificent beeches and yews, and roamed by many kinds of wildlife including deer. The views from the house itself were beautiful.

Despite the ideal and the idyll, the experiment in the end was a failure. The school never paid for itself, and Russell's writing of popular books and journalism, and his crossings and recrossings of the Atlantic to make lecture tours—he hated the sea journeys— were mainly aimed at subsidizing it. Dora also made a lecture tour to America, but her chief responsibility was running the school. Staff proved a difficulty, Russell and Dora never found teachers who could consistently apply their principles, which involved allowing freedom with discipline—for despite allegations to the contrary, Russell's school was not an anarchy of infants; he later wrote, 'To let the children go free was to establish a reign of terror, in which the strong kept the weak trembling and miserable. A school is like the world: only government can prevent brutal violence.'

Another difficulty was that the school attracted a high proportion of problem children, whose parents had tried to send them elsewhere but had been driven at last to try experimental schools. Because the Russells needed the money they accepted these children, only to find that they made running the school very difficult.

Worst of all, however, was the effect on Russell's own children. The other pupils thought they were unduly favoured, because their parents ran the school; but in an effort to be fair, Russell and Dora tried to treat them on the same footing as the others, with the consequence that John and Kate were effectively deprived of their parents, and suffered for it. The early happiness in the family was, in Russell's own words, thereby 'destroyed, and was replaced by awkwardness and embarrassment' (*A* 390).

Hopes for education as a way of transforming the world were widespread in the years after the First World War. In Austria, for example, where the demise of the Austro-Hungarian Empire had had a shattering effect, many young intellectuals took up schoolteaching in the hope of building mankind anew. Karl Popper and Ludwig Wittgenstein were among them. In an indirect way Russell was part of this movement. But the realities of teaching, and the

15

sheer intractibility of human material, quickly disillusioned most of them, and they gave it up.

In 1931 Russell's brother Frank died suddenly, and Russell inherited the earldom. With it he inherited his brother's debts and an obligation to pay £400 a year in alimony to the second of his brother's three ex-wives. His attitude to the earldom was somewhat wry, but he was not averse to making use of it in various ways, not least in exploiting the automatic entry it gave him to Establishment platforms, where his expression of iconoclastic and independent views could have the greatest effect. Nevertheless he did not often attend the House of Lords, and preserved a healthy streak of contempt for the British class system.

At about this time Russell's marriage was feeling the strain both of the school and of the various affairs which both spouses allowed themselves. Russell did not object to Dora having affairs, but he did not wish to be responsible for any children that resulted. Dora became pregnant by an American lover, and the child was at first registered as Russell's; later, when he saw her listed in Debrett's as one of his offspring, he instituted proceedings to have her name removed. To this extent, therefore, Russell had dynastic impulses.

In the aftermath of the school and separation from Dora, and with the additional financial burdens inherited from his brother, Russell was still under the necessity of making a living from his pen. A lucrative association with the Hearst newspapers in America, for which Russell had written a column, came to an end early in the decade, so Russell had to devote his energies to books. In 1932 he published *The Scientific Outlook*, and in 1934 one of his best books, a work of political history called *Freedom and Organization 1814–1914*. In 1935 he published *In Praise of Idleness* and in 1936 *Which Way to Peace?* In this book he reasserted his qualified pacifism and his commitment to the idea of world government. But by the time this book was published he had already come to feel the need for even deeper qualifications of pacifism, especially—as events in Germany over the previous two or three years showed—in the face of such an 'utterly revolting' threat as he perceived in Nazism. By the outbreak of the Second World War he had decided that resistance to Hitler must be unequivocal.

In 1937 Russell published *The Amberley Papers*, a three-volume record of the life of his parents. He found this work 'restful', because he admired and profoundly agreed with his parents' radical views, and felt nostalgia for the more hopeful and spacious world—so it seemed to Russell—in which they had fought for them. In working both on this book and on *Freedom and Organization* Russell had the assistance of a young woman who had previously taught at his school, and who had become first his lover and then, in 1936, his third wife: Patricia (commonly called 'Peter') Spence. In 1937 they had a son, Conrad. They moved to a house near Oxford where Russell gave a course of lectures and held discussions with some of the younger philosophers, among them A. J. Ayer. He published *Power, A New Social Analysis* in 1938, and his Oxford lectures, at first entitled 'Words and Facts', became his next philosophical book, *An Inquiry into Meaning and Truth*, published in 1940.

In 1938 Russell went with Peter and Conrad to America to take up an appointment as visiting professor at the University of Chicago. Although he had stimulating conversations there with brilliant students and colleagues—among the latter Rudolf Carnap—he did not get on with the head of the philosophy department, and he disliked Chicago, which he described as 'a beastly town with vile weather'. At the end of the year the Russells went to California, where the weather proved altogether more congenial. Russell taught at the University of California at Los Angeles (UCLA). In the summer of 1939 John and Kate came to spend a Californian holiday, but the outbreak of war made it impossible for them to return to England, so Russell placed them both in UCLA.

Despite the sunshine he was less happy at UCLA than he had been at Chicago, because the staff and students were not very able and the President of the University seemed to Russell especially disagreeable. After a year, therefore, he accepted an invitation to become a professor at the City College of New York. But before he could assume his post a scandal was raised against him on the grounds of irreligion and immorality. It was started by an Episcopalian bishop, carried forward enthusiastically by Catholics, and achieved focus in a legal suit brought by the mother of an intending female student of the College. The mother, a Mrs Kay, said that Russell's presence in the College would be dangerous to her daughter's virtue. Russell was unable to plead in court because the suit was brought against the Municipality of New York and he was not himself a party to it. Mrs Kay's lawyer described Russell's works as 'lecherous, libidinous, lustful, venerous, erotomaniac, aphrodisiac, irreverent, narrow-minded, untruthful, and bereft of moral fibre'. One of the grounds for this was that Russell had stated in a book that very young children should not be punished for masturbating. The Irish Catholic judge was even more vituperative in his summing up against Russell than Mrs Kay's lawyer had been. Mrs Kay, naturally, won.

The case raised not just the whole of New York City and State against Russell, but the whole country. Driven from his New York job, he could at first find nowhere else that would give him a teaching post, and no newspaper that would offer him a column. Because of war conditions it was impossible to get money from England. He was thus stranded abroad without a livelihood, and with a family to support.

Russell was rescued from this dilemma first by Harvard University, which generously invited him to lecture in 1940, and then by a Philadelphia millionaire, Dr Barnes, a passionate collector of art who had established a Foundation for the study chiefly of art history. He gave Russell a five-year contract to lecture at the Foundation. To his amusement, and despite thinking it incongruous with academic philosophy, Russell gave his lectures in a room hung with French paintings of nudes. Barnes was something of an eccentric with a reputation for falling out with his staff; less than halfway through Russell's term he suddenly issued a dismissal notice on the grounds that, in his opinion, Russell's lectures were poorly prepared. These lectures were subsequently published as *A History of Western Philosophy*, by far Russell's most successful book from a popular and financial point of view. Russell sued for breach of contract, and gave the manuscript to the judge to read. He won his case. It must be said that parts of this famous book are sketchy enough to make one feel a certain sympathy with the Philadelphia millionaire. But in other respects it is a marvellously readable, magnificently sweeping survey of Western thought, distinctive for placing it informatively into its historical context. Russell enjoyed writing it, and the enjoyment shows; his later remarks about it equally show that he was conscious of its shortcomings.

Work on the *History* was continued in the library of Bryn Mawr College after Russell's break with Barnes. This was owing to the kindness of Professor Paul Weiss who invited Russell there while he awaited permission from the British Embassy in Washington to return to England. Trinity College had offered Russell a Fellowship, which, together with a handsome advance for the *History*, rescued Russell from his difficulties. Just before sailing home through the dangers of German submarines in the Atlantic, Russell spent a short time at Princeton, where he had discussions with Einstein, Kurt Gödel, and Wolfgang Pauli.

For the next few years Russell taught in Cambridge, publishing the *History* in 1945 and *Human Knowledge: Its Scope and Limits* in 1948. This was Russell's last great work of philosophy, and he was disappointed when it received little notice from the philosophical community. One reason for this he attributed to the considerable vogue then and for some time afterwards enjoyed by Wittgenstein's ideas. In 1949, a year which he described as the 'apogee of his respectability', his Fellowship at Trinity was changed to a Fellowship for life without teaching duties; he was elected to an Honorary Fellowship of the British Academy; the BBC invited him to give the first ever series of Reith Lectures; King George VI gave him the Order of Merit; and in the following year he was awarded the Nobel Prize for Literature, news of which reached him while he was on yet another visit to the United States.

Russell was pleased to be given the OM, and went to Buckingham Palace for the investiture. King George was embarrassed at having to behave graciously to an iconoclastic ex-convict adulterer, who in addition was—in his own words—so 'queer looking', so he said, 'You have sometimes behaved in a way which would not do if generally adopted.' The reply that sprang to Russell's lips, but which he managed to suppress, was, 'Like your brother', meaning the abdicated Edward VIII; instead he said, 'How a man should behave depends upon his profession. A postman, for instance, should knock at all the doors in a street at which he has letters to deliver, but if anybody else knocked on all the doors, he would be considered a public nuisance.' The King hastily changed the subject (*A* 516–17).

Russell's new respectability, and in particular his long-standing opposition to the communism of the Soviet Union, made him

useful to the British Government in the deepening chill of the
Cold War. In this capacity he visited Germany and Sweden to
lecture, on the latter occasion being involved in a seaplane crash
in Trondheim harbour, which necessitated his having to swim
to safety through freezing water; and on the former being tem-
porarily made a member of the British Armed Forces, to his great
amusement.

Russell travelled widely in the 1950s—to Australia, to India, to
America again, as well as to continental Europe and Scandinavia
—lecturing all the while, and enjoying considerable celebrity.
Three years after separating from Peter Spence he married his
long-standing American friend, Edith Finch, and they made a
honeymoon to Paris; but even on sightseeing jaunts around the
city—which neither had ever explored as tourists, for the good
reason that both had previously lived there—Russell was recognized and crowds clustered round him.

Travelling and lecturing, as always with Russell, turned into
books. The Reith Lectures appeared as *Authority and the Individual*. In 1954 he published *Human Society in Ethics and Politics*, which included his Nobel Prize oration. Because his Nobel
Prize was for Literature (the citation nominated *Marriage and
Morals*) Russell was prompted to write fiction. In 1912 he had
written a novel but not attempted to publish it; now he wrote
two collections of short stories—more accurately: fables, all with
philosophical or polemical intent—called *Satan in the Suburbs*
and *Nightmares of Eminent Persons*. In 1956 he published *Portraits From Memory*, a series of sketches of eminent people he
had known, and in 1959 he gave the world his intellectual autobiography, *My Philosophical Development*, which summarizes the
progress of his views from childhood onwards.

But any idea that Russell had finally entered the Establishment fold, and would subside into grandly respectable and quies-
cent old age, was mistaken; for Russell saw that the world was
beset by a horrifying and rapidly growing danger which he felt it
imperative to resist. This was the proliferation of weapons of mass
destruction. From the mid-1950s until his death in February 1970
he campaigned against weapons and war with the passion of a
young man, among other things earning another prison sentence—
commuted, in the light of his great age (he was by then in his

nineties), to a week in a prison hospital—and in his very last years again earning dislike and hostility, especially for what seemed to be intemperate, ill-judged, and even hysterical opposition to American actions in the Vietnam War. It later transpired that his accusations of war crimes against the United States were based on largely correct information. In the course of these endeavours Russell became the first president of the Campaign for Nuclear Disarmament (CND), published two books—*Common Sense and Nuclear Warfare* and *Has Man A Future?*—and was instrumental in establishing the Pugwash Conference and later, with Jean-Paul Sartre, the International War Crimes Tribunal in opposition to the Vietnam War.

The political struggles of Russell's last fifteen years are canvassed in Chapter 4 below. By the close of his life, despite bodily age and some infirmity (but he was spry and alert until the end, dying in his ninety-eighth year) Russell seemed to have grown younger with time; his grandmother sent him into the world a middle-aged Victorian, and he metamorphosed into an eternally young knight-errant: honest, indomitable, equipped with a formidable intellect and great ability as a writer, who used his gift—not least among them his extraordinarily incisive powers of reason and wit—to do battle with dragons.

The perspective of time either enlarges or diminishes those who have occupied the public view. Most dwindle into foothills (which is to say, footnotes); a few rise to Himalayan majesty. Among their peaks Russell stands high.

2 Logic and Philosophy

Introduction

By his own account, Russell's chief philosophical motive was to find out if anything can be known with certainty. This ambition, identical to that of Descartes, had risen in him as a result of two early intellectual crises: his loss of religious faith, and his disappointment at having to accept unproven axioms as the basis of geometry. His first truly original philosophical endeavour was to show that mathematics rests on logic. Success in this enterprise would have provided a grounding of certainty for mathematical knowledge. The project failed, but a number of important philosophical advances came out of the attempt. Russell then turned to the problems of general philosophy, where certainty is even harder to find. He worked at constructing theories which he hoped would, despite the elusiveness of certainty, provide satisfactory solutions nevertheless. He returned to these problems again and again, developing and changing his views but keeping faith with the analytical techniques derived from his logical work. He felt able, in the end, to claim a measure of success, although he knew that few of his fellow philosophers agreed with him.

When one surveys Russell's philosophical work, ignoring the fact that it evolved over a very long span, frequently and lengthily interrupted by many other activities, one is surprised at how continuous and logical an evolution it represents. In his own account of his philosophical development Russell states that his philosophical life divides into two, the first part consisting in an early and short-lived flirtation with idealism, the second, inspired by his discovery of new logical techniques, dominating his outlook from then on:

There is one major division in my philosophical work; in the years 1899–1900 I adopted the philosophy of logical atomism and the technique of Peano in mathematical logic. This was so great a revolution as to make my previous work, except such as was purely mathematical, irrelevant to everything that I did later. The change in these years was a revolution; subsequent changes have been in the nature of an evolution. (*MPD* 11)

The evolution that followed the revolution was considerable, but at every point it was driven by a need to solve problems thrown up by preceding phases, or, if the problems were too great, to find alternative routes forward. This dialectical continuity of concerns shows that Charles Broad's witticism, 'Mr Bertrand Russell produces a new system of philosophy each year or so, and Mr G. E. Moore none at all', although perhaps true of Moore, is not true of Russell, least of all in its hint that there was something capricious about the steps in Russell's philosophical pilgrimage.

In the years between taking his degree and discovering Peano—roughly, the decade of the 1890s—Russell was under the influence of German idealism as favoured by his teachers at Cambridge. The published version of his Fellowship dissertation was a Kantian account of geometry, but his main allegiance was to Hegel. He wrote a Hegelian account of number, and planned a complete idealist dialectic of the sciences aimed at proving, in Hegel's style, that all reality is mental.

Russell later dismissed this work, with characteristic robustness, as 'nothing but unmitigated rubbish' (*MPD* 32). The revolution in his philosophical approach occurred, as we have seen, as a result of his joint revolt against idealism with Moore, and his discovery of the logical work of Peano. This last was particularly significant, because it galvanized Russell's ambition to derive mathematics from logic, and offered the means of doing so. The years between 1900 and 1910 were principally devoted to this task, much valuable philosophical work arising in the process. The project is mooted in *The Principles of Mathematics* (1903), and the detailed attempt to carry it out constitutes *Principia Mathematica* (1910–13). Among the classic philosophical papers produced by Russell on the way is 'On Denoting' (1905), some of the ideas in which have been immensely influential in the subsequent history of philosophy

The philosophical work of these years continued after the associated logical work was brought to an end by the publication of *Principia Mathematica*. Russell set about applying the techniques of analysis developed in this work to the problems of metaphysics (enquiry into the nature of reality) and epistemology (enquiry into how we get and test knowledge). His enduring little classic, *The Problems of Philosophy* (1912) sketches the metaphysical and epistemological views he then held. He proposed to give them more detailed treatment in subsequent writings, and began in 1913 by drafting a large book, posthumously published as *Theory of Knowledge* (1984). But he was dissatisfied with aspects of it, so instead of publishing it in book form he broke it up and published part of it as a series of papers. At the same time a suggestion by Whitehead inspired him to apply logical techniques to the analysis of perception; the result was a set of lectures delivered at Harvard and subsequently published as *Our Knowledge of the External World* (1914). This book, together with a paper entitled 'The Relation of Sense-Data to Physics' published in the same year, represents an excursus by Russell into something like phenomenalism. 'Phenomenalism' is the view that perceptual knowledge can be analysed in terms of our acquaintance with the fundamental data of sensory experience. (I say 'something like phenomenalism' because although Russell half a century later described these views as phenomenalistic, in the original writings they are not unambiguously so; this point is discussed in the appropriate place below.) Four years later, in another series of lectures, Russell applied his analytic method to objects and our talk of them. He called this the 'Philosophy of Logical Atomism'. At the same time he published what is in effect a popular version of *Principia Mathematica*, setting out the basic ideas of the philosophy of mathematics. This book is entitled *An Introduction to Mathematical Philosophy* (1918).

In the 1920s Russell sought to extend and improve the application of his analytic techniques to the philosophy of psychology and physics. The first fruit of this was *The Analysis of Mind* (1921) in which his version of quasi-phenomenalism is applied to the analysis of mental entities. The second was *The Analysis of Matter* (1927), where Russell seeks to analyse the chief concepts of physics, such as force and matter, in terms of events. The argument of this book is strongly realist; Russell did not think it feasible to analyse the basic concepts of physics without admitting that certain entities exist independently of perception of them, which marked the end of any dalliance with phenomenalism. It might also be described as a 'return' to realism, because Russell had been committed to a rather swingeing form of realism before writing *Our Knowledge of the External World*.

Having made this return journey from a version of phenom-enalism or something close to it, Russell reconsidered problems which he now felt had not been properly dealt with under his phenomenalist assumptions. The result was *An Inquiry Into Meaning and Truth* (1940) where he again discusses the relation of experience to contingent knowledge, and *Human Knowledge* (1948), where, among other things, he returns to a matter left in-adequately discussed in earlier writings: the important question of non-demonstrative (non-deductive) inference, of the kind gener-ally supposed to be employed in science.

Each of these phases in the development of Russell's thought merits extended discussion, to be found in the works cited in Fur-ther Reading below. In the following sections I give a summary account of them.

The Rejection of Idealism

Idealism takes a number of variant forms, but its basic tenet is that reality is fundamentally mental. 'Idea-ism' would be a more informative version of the name. It is a technical term of philo-sophy, and has nothing to do with ordinary senses of the English word 'ideal'. In one of its forms, as held by Bishop Berkeley, ideal-ism is the thesis that reality ultimately consists of a community of minds and their ideas. One of the minds is infinite, and causes most of the ideas; Berkeley identifies it as God. In later views of the kind espoused by T. H. Green and F. H. Bradley, both of whom were much influenced by German idealism, the thesis is that the universe ultimately consists of a single Mind which, so to speak, experiences itself. They argue that our finite, partial, and individual experience, which tells us that the world consists of a plurality of independently existing entities—many if not most of which are material rather than mental—is contradictory or at very least misleading. This plurality of things is mere 'appear-ance', which obscures rather than represents the true nature of reality. This implies an important concomitant of the idealist view, as Russell had learned to accept it: that because plurality is a misleading appearance, the truth is that everything is related to everything else in the universe, and therefore the universe is ultimately a single thing—everything is One. This view is called 'monism'.

When Moore and Russell rejected idealism in 1898 (the event was marked by publication in that year of Moore's article 'The Nature of Judgment') they opposed both of the chief theses of idealism: that experience and its objects are inextricably mutually dependent, and that everything is one. They thereby committed themselves to 'realism', which is the thesis that the objects of experience are independent of experience of them, and to 'pluralism', which is the thesis that there are many independent things in the world.

Russell saw idealism and its concomitant monism as arising from a view about *relations* which, once refuted, opens the way to pluralist realism. Relations are expressed by such sentences as 'A is to the left of B', 'A is earlier than B', 'A loves B'. On the idealist view, Russell claimed, all relations are 'internal', that is, they are properties of the terms they relate, and, in a full description, appear as properties of the whole which they form with their relata. This is sometimes plausible; in 'A loves B' A's loving B is a property of A—that is, is a fact about the nature of A—and the complex fact denoted by 'A loves B' has the property of being a *loving-of-B-by-A*. But if all relations are internal it immediately follows that the universe constitutes what the idealist philosopher Harold Joachim calls 'a significant whole', for it means that it is part of the nature of anything to be related to everything else, and that therefore a full description of any one thing will tell us everything about the whole universe, and vice versa. Bradley puts the point like this: 'Reality is one. It must be single because plurality, taken as real, contradicts itself. Plurality implies relations, and, through its relations it unwillingly asserts always a superior unity' (*Appearance and Reality*, 519).

In opposition to this view Russell argued that the idealists commit a fundamental mistake. This is that they take all propositions to be of subject-predicate form. Consider the sentence 'The ball is round'. This can be used to express a proposition in which the property of roundness is predicated of a given ball ('predicated' means: applied to, said of). In Russell's view, the idealists wrongly took it that all propositions, even relational ones, are ultimately of subject-predicate form, which means that every proposition must, in the final analysis, constitute a predication on reality as a whole, and that relations as such are unreal. For example: on the idealist view the proposition 'A is to the left of B' should properly be understood as saying, 'Reality has the property of A-appearing-to-be-to-the-left-of-B' (or something like this).

But if one sees that many propositions are irreducibly relational in form, one thereby sees that monism is false. To say that many propositions are irreducibly relational is to say that relations are real or 'external'—they are not grounded in the terms they relate; the relation 'to the left of' does not belong intrinsically to any spatial object, which is to say that no spatial object must of necessity be to the left of other things. For it to be true that 'A is to the left of B', Russell argued, there therefore has to be an A *and separately* a B for the former to stand to the latter in the relation 'left of'. And of course to say that there are more things than one is to reject monism.

Rejection of monism constitutes a rejection of idealism for Russell because it is crucial to idealism that the relation of experience to its objects should be internal, which is in effect to say that there is no such relation; which is again in effect to say that relations are unreal. But on Russell's opposed view that relations are real, experience cannot be conflated with its objects; which is to say that those objects exist independently of being experienced. And this is central to what Russell and Moore meant by realism.

It is disputable whether Russell is right in thinking that all the idealists (including Leibniz), and before them the Schoolmen with their metaphysics of substance and attribute, were committed to the view that all propositions are subject-predicate in form. But he certainly took himself to have discovered a highly important flaw in previous philosophy. With the rejection of idealism he went for a time to the other extreme, that of being a realist about everything. By his own account he was a 'naïve realist' in the sense of one who believes that all the perceived properties of material objects are genuine properties of them, a physical realist in believing that all the theoretical entities of physics are 'actually existing entities' (*MPD* 48–9), and a Platonic realist in believing also in the existence, or at least in the 'being' (where this is a qualified and perhaps lesser kind of existence), of 'numbers, the Homeric gods, relations, chimeras, and four-dimensional spaces' *The Principles of Mathematics* (*PoM* 449). Russell later trimmed this luxuriant universe by applying 'Ockham's razor', the principle that entities should not be multiplied unnecessarily. For example, if physical objects can be exhaustively explained in terms of subatomic entities, then a basic inventory of the universe should not contain *both* trees *and* the quarks, leptons, and gauge particles of which trees are made. This, later, was how he applied the technique of analysis. But he still believed in an inclusive realism in *PoM*, to which he turned after encountering the work of Giuseppe Peano in Paris in 1900.

The Foundations of Mathematics

Leibniz had dreamed of a *characteristica universalis*, a universal and completely precise language, use of which will solve all philosophical problems. Russell recognized, in his book on Leibniz, that this was a desire for a symbolic logic, by which Russell then meant the 'Boolean algebra' developed by George Boole in the mid-nineteenth century. But at that juncture he did not think Leibniz was right to suppose that philosophical problems can be solved by employing the technicalities of a deductive logical system, for the reason that the truly important questions of philosophy are about matters that are 'anterior to deduction', namely, the concepts or facts referred to in the premises from which inference starts. Whatever these are, Russell argued, they are not supplied to us by logic; logic can only help us in reasoning about them.

But Russell changed his mind when he encountered Peano's work. Peano's advances in logical technique (they had been anticipated by Gottlob Frege, but neither Peano nor Russell then realized this) immediately suggested to Russell ways of stating the fundamental principles of logic, and of showing two centrally important things: first, how all the concepts of mathematics can be defined in terms of them, and secondly, how all mathematical truths can be proved from them. In short, it suggested to Russell how to show that logic and mathematics are identical. This is the aim of both *PoM*, and its more fully worked out version, *Principia Mathematica* (*PM*).

The project of deriving mathematics from logic is known as 'logicism'. In *PoM* Russell did not attempt a rigorous assault on this part of the programme, limiting himself instead to an informal sketch. The rigorous assault was left to *PM*. Chief among Russell's reasons for delaying the task until *PM* was his discovery of a paradox which threatened the whole enterprise.

Russell's first task was to define the concepts of mathematics using as small a number as possible of purely logical notions. (Here follow three paragraphs of informal technicality, which need not detain the reader.) Letting 'p' and 'q' stand for propositions, these notions are: negation (not-p), disjunction (p or q), conjunction (p and q), and implication (if p then q). To these operations are added symbols for representing the inner structure of propositions: 'Fx' is a functional expression in which 'x' is a variable standing for any individual, and 'F' is a predicate letter standing for any property. Thus 'Fx' says that x is F (an instance of what it symbolizes is: 'the tree is tall'). One of the important technical advances that Russell was able to use is a way of *quantifying* such functions. Using notation which is now standard in logic, quantification is expressed like this: (x) expresses 'all xs', so (x)Fx says that *all* xs are F, (∃x) expresses 'at least one x', so (∃x)Fx says that *at least one* x is F. And finally there is the notion of identity: 'a = b' says that a and b are not two objects but one and the same object. With this simple language it is possible to define the concepts of mathematics.

Earlier mathematicians had investigated the relations among mathematical notions and had recognized that they are all reducible to the natural numbers (the counting numbers 1, 2, 3 . . .), although no one had so far demonstrated this precisely. The first step in the programme was therefore to define the natural numbers in logical terms. This is what Frege had already done, although Russell did not at the time realize this.

The definition exploits the notion of classes: 2 is defined as the class of all couples, 3 as the class of all trios, and so on. In turn, a 'couple' is defined as a class having members x and y where x and y are not identical and where, if there is any other member z of the class, z is identical with either x or y. The general definition of number is stated in terms of sets of similar classes, where 'similarity' is a precise notion denoting a one–one relation:

two classes are similar if a one–one relation is specifiable as holding between their members.

With these notions in place, a raft of problems is solved, among them: how to define 0 and 1 (Russell pointed out that these are two of the most difficult notions in mathematics), how to overcome 'one and many' puzzles (how many things is a chair: is it one, or—if you count its parts and constituents—many?), and how to understand infinite numbers. Once the whole numbers are defined, the others (positive and negative numbers, fractions, real numbers, complex numbers) present relatively little difficulty.

The first part of the programme—defining mathematical concepts in terms of logical ones—therefore seems largely unproblematic, once the right technicalities are available. The second—the distinctively logicist part of showing that mathematical truths can be proved from the fundamental principles of logic—turns out to be vastly more difficult.

The main reason for this, from Russell's point of view at the time, was his discovery of paradox. The paradox relates to a notion which, as the foregoing sketch shows, is central to the project: the notion of classes. In the course of his work Russell was led to ponder the fact that some classes are, and some are not, members of themselves. For example, the class of teaspoons is not a teaspoon, and therefore is not a member of itself; but the class of things which are not teaspoons is a member of itself because it is not a teaspoon. What, then, of the class of all those classes which are not members of themselves? If this class is not a member of itself, then by definition it is a member of itself; and if it is a member of itself, then by definition it is not a member of itself. So it is both a member of itself and not a member of itself. Thus paradox.

At first Russell thought that some trivial mistake was to blame, but after much effort to put things right, and after consulting Frege and Whitehead, it became clear to him that disaster had struck. Russell published *PoM* without having found a remedy. But by the time he and Whitehead came to write *PM* he had, he thought, found a way out—but his strategy proved highly controversial. Matters can be described as follows.

The attempt to deduce the theorems of mathematics from purely logical axioms cannot proceed, Russell found, without supplementary axioms to make possible the task of proving certain theorems in arithmetic and set theory. Two of these supplementary axioms (their details do not matter; I mention them for completeness) are the 'axiom of infinity', which states that there are infinite collections in the world, and the 'axiom of choice' (sometimes called the 'multiplicative axiom') which states that for every set of disjoint non-empty sets there is a set which shares exactly one member with each of the member sets. The axioms are needed so that numbers can be defined in terms of classes, as sketched above. But they both appear to involve a difficulty, which is that they are existential in character, that is, they say '*there is* such-and-such'—in the first case, a number, in the second, a set— and this is a problem because logic should not be concerned with what does or does not exist, but only with purely formal matters. But Russell found a solution: it is to treat mathematical sentences as conditionals, that is, as sentences of 'if—then—' form, with the axioms occupying the 'if' gap: as such they say, 'if you premiss this axiom, then—'. Because these conditionals are themselves derivable from the axioms of logic, the apparent importation of existential considerations does not matter.

But much greater difficulty arose with a third supplementary axiom, the 'axiom of reducibility'. This is the axiom Russell adopted to overcome the paradox problem, but which other logicians find hard to accept.

The axiom of reducibility is tied to Russell's 'theory of types'. An informal way of understanding this theory is to note that the paradox discovered by Russell arises because the property of not-being-a-member-of-itself is applied to the class of all classes having that property. If a restriction could be introduced which ruled that this property is applicable only to the member classes and not to the class of those classes, the paradox would not arise. This suggests that there should be something like a distinction of levels among properties, such that those attributed at one level are not attributable at a higher level.

There is a version of type theory—it is a simpler version than Russell's—which captures this intuition and seems plausible to some logicians. It was suggested by the mathematician-philosopher Frank Ramsey and is called the 'simple theory of types'. It puts matters like this: the language which applies to a given domain has level 1 expressions—names—which refer to objects in the domain, and it has level 2 expressions—predicates—which refer only to properties of those objects, and it has level 3 expressions—predicates of predicates—which refer only to properties of those properties . . . and so on. The rule is that every expression belongs to a particular type and can only be applied to expressions of the next type below it in the hierarchy. In line with the informal sketch just given, one sees how this strategy suggests a solution to the paradox problem.

Russell's more complicated version of type theory is called the 'ramified theory of types'. (The correct way to understand this theory is a matter of controversy—see, for example, Hylton 1990, chapter 7—but the following sketch can serve as a first approximation.) Russell's reason for introducing 'ramification'—which means the internal subdivision of types into 'orders'—was that he thought a solution to the paradox problem specifically needed it. He took it that the paradox problem results from attempting to define properties by means of expressions which contain reference to 'all properties', so talk of 'all properties' must be strictly controlled. Properties of, say, type 1 are therefore to be subdivided into orders: a first order of properties in whose definition the expression 'all properties' does not occur; a second order of properties in whose definition the expression 'all properties of the first order' occurs; a third order in whose definition 'all properties of the second order' occurs; and so on. Since there is never reference to 'all properties' which does not anchor it to a definite order, no property is ever defined in such a way that reference is made to the totality it belongs to. And this avoids paradox.

But it does so at a major cost. It introduces difficulties into the theory of real numbers by blocking its most important definitions and theorems. It was to overcome this problem that Russell introduced the axiom of reducibility, which tries to engineer a way of reducing orders within a type to the lowest order. This manoeuvre, likened by one commentator to using 'brute force' to salvage real number theory, was abandoned by Russell in the second edition of *PM* (1927). But because he could not accept that there is any alternative to a ramified theory of types he was left in quandary. It was in response to this that Ramsey put forward the 'simple' theory of types sketched above. (It is as well to note that

Ramsey's theory invites debate on its own account. It makes the controversial claim that the circularity in definitions which ascribe properties to themselves is harmless; and it demands an equally controversial realism about the existence of totalities before they are defined.)

Russell's logicist ambitions ran into difficulties partly on their own account and partly because, as later developments in mathematics—especially the work of Kurt Gödel—suggest, logicism itself is unfeasible. Gödel showed that in any formal system adequate for number theory there is an undecidable formula, that is, a formula such that neither it nor its negation can be proved. A corollary of this is that the consistency of such a system cannot be established within the system, so one cannot assume that mathematics (or anyway large parts of it) can be provided with a set of axioms sufficient for generating all its truths. His work shows that the axiomatic method has profound inherent limitations, and that the only way to prove the consistency of many kinds of deductive systems is to use a system of reasoning so complicated that its own consistency is equally doubtful.

What Russell required to see his logicist project through was a formal systematization which excludes the possibility of contradiction. Gödel's work says this is impossible. It has to be concluded that the achievement of *PoM* and particularly *PM* is not to be found in the degree to which they realize their stated aims, but in what might be called their many significant 'spin-offs' for logic and philosophy.

The Theory of Descriptions

One of the most influential spin-offs was Russell's 'Theory of Descriptions'. In working out this important theory Russell achieved a number of different goals. One lesson he had learned from arguing against idealism is that the surface grammar of language can mislead us about the meaning of what we say. As noted above, he thought that the reason philosophers had been led into adopting a metaphysics of substance and attribute—a view that, as debate in the history of philosophy shows, runs into deep difficulties—was that they had taken all propositions to be fundamentally subject-predicate in form. 'The table is made of wood' and 'the table is to the left of the door' were both treated as having the expression 'the table' as subject, and as predicate the expressions which in each case follow the copula 'is'. But whereas the first sentence might express a proposition of that form, the second expresses something quite different, namely, a relational proposition: it in fact has two subjects ('the table' and 'the door') and it asserts that they stand in a particular relation to one another. So the logical form of the second sentence is quite different from the logical form of the first. In Russell's view, the need, therefore, is for a method of revealing the true underlying form of what we say to help us avoid philosophical mistakes.

The next important step Russell took was to apply the new logic to this task. Just as it serves to define the concepts and operations of mathematics, so we can use it to analyse what we say about the world, thus getting a correct picture of reality.

One way of showing how the theory of descriptions carries out this task is to describe how it solves an important problem about meaning and reference. The background to Russell's treatment of this problem is to be found in the work of Alexius Meinong, an Austrian philosopher whose writings Russell had carefully studied and who had therefore been an early influence on him. Meinong held that denoting expressions—names like 'Russell' and descriptions like 'the author of *The Principles of Mathematics*'—can occur significantly in propositions (strictly: in sentences expressing propositions) only if what they denote exists. Suppose, Meinong argued, you say, 'the golden mountain does not exist'. Obviously, you are talking about something—the golden mountain—when you assert that it does not exist; and since what you say is meaningful, there must therefore in some sense *be* a golden mountain. His theory is that everything that can be talked about—named, referred to—must therefore either exist or have some kind of 'being' even if such being does not amount to existence, for otherwise what we say would be meaningless.

Russell accepted this view at first, and indeed held it in *PoM*; which is why, as noted earlier, he there expressed belief in the existence or at least being of 'numbers, Homeric gods and chimeras'. But the implausibility of this view soon came to offend his 'vivid sense of reality', as he put it, for it crowded the universe not just with abstract and mythological entities but also with *impossible* objects like 'the round square'—and this Russell could not accept.

Russell used the techniques of logic to devise a beautiful solution. He did not wish to give up the view that a name is meaningful only if there is something it names, but he argued that the only 'logically proper' names are those which denote *particular* entities with which one can be *acquainted*. By 'acquaintance' Russell meant an immediate and direct relation between a mind and an object; examples include awareness of sense-data in perception (see pp. 40–1 below) and knowledge of such abstract entities as propositions. Only logically proper names can properly occupy subject-position in sentences. The best examples are the demonstrative pronouns *this* and *that*, for the reason that they are guaranteed a reference every time they are used. All other apparent naming expressions are in fact not naming expressions at all; they are—or when they are analysed they turn out to be—'definite descriptions', that is, expressions of the form 'the so-and-so'. The importance of this is that when sentences containing descriptions are analysed, the descriptive phrases vanish, and therefore the meaningfulness of what one says does not depend upon the supposed existence or being of some entity which the descriptions appear—according to surface grammar—to denote.

This can be seen by considering an example. Take the sentence 'The present king of France is bald', said at a time when France has no king. On the supposition that sentences are always either true or false, what is one to say if asked: is this sentence true or false? It seems obvious to say 'false'—not because the present king of France has a fine head of hair, but because he does not exist. This point gave Russell his clue. He argued that sentences with definite descriptions in grammatical subject-place turn out upon analysis to be shorthand for a set of sentences asserting the existence, the uniqueness, and the baldness of something having the property of being the present king of France. Thus 'the present king of France is bald' is equivalent to:

(1) there is a king of France,
(2) there is not more than one king of France,
(3) whatever is king of France is bald.

Sentence (1) is an existence claim; (2) is a uniqueness claim, that is, it captures the implication of 'the' in the description that there is only one thing being talked about; and (3) is the predication. The original sentence 'the present king of France is bald' is true when all three are true; it is false if any one of them is false. In the present case it is false because (1) is false.

In none of (1)–(3) does the description 'the present king of France' appear. Because the descriptive phrase has vanished—has been analysed away—there is no need to invoke a subsistent king of France to make the sentence meaningful.

Owing to the imperfections of ordinary language, and the fact that the surface forms of sentences can diverge from their underlying logical form, the analysis thus given is not yet, says Russell, good enough. It needs to be expressed in the 'perfect language' of symbolic logic. This alone can display with *complete* clarity what is being asserted by 'the present king of France is bald.' In notation which is now standard, the logical analysis of this sentence is:

$$(\exists x)[Fx \,\&\, (y)(Fy \rightarrow y = x) \,\&\, Gx]$$

The '&' in this string of symbols stands for 'and', dividing the string of symbols into three conjoined formulae, so the three sentences (1)–(3) above are respectively:

(1) $(\exists x)Fx$

This is pronounced 'there is an x such that x is F'. Let 'F' be 'has the property of being king of France'; the formula symbolizes 'there is something which is king of France'. (The existential quantifier $(\exists x)$ binds every occurrence of 'x' in the whole string, of course, as the square brackets show.)

(2) $(y)(Fy \rightarrow y = x)$

This is pronounced 'for everything y, if y is F then y and x are identical'. This expresses the uniqueness implied by 'the', that is, that only one thing has the property F.

(3) Gx.

This is pronounced 'x is G'. Let 'G' be 'is bald'; the formula symbolizes 'x is bald'.

Objections to Russell's theory mainly take the form of resisting his claim that definite descriptions are never referring expressions, and questioning his analysis of sentences containing them in grammatical subject-place. In the latter connection, what some dispute is the claim that definite descriptions embody both uniqueness and existence claims.

The problem about uniqueness is exemplified by someone's saying, 'the baby is crying'. Russell's analysis seems to imply that this can only be true if there is just one baby in the world. The way out is to require that there is an implicit understanding that the context of the remark shows how much of the world is included in its range of application. Suppose the parents of a baby inhabit a block of flats where there are dozens of babies, all crying, and their own begins to follow suit. If one said, 'the baby is crying', there would obviously be no misunderstanding because the context restricts reference to the one baby in which they have a special interest. So much seems intuitive, and suggests ways of disposing of the objection by appealing to implicit or explicit delimitations of the 'domain of discourse'.

The problem about existence is a little more complex. In a much-cited discussion of Russell's theory, P. F. Strawson argues that in saying 'the present king of France is bald' one is not *stating* that a present king of France exists, but presupposing or assuming that it does ('On Referring', *Mind*, 1950). This is shown by the fact that if someone uttered this sentence, his interlocutors are not likely to say, 'that's false', but instead, 'there's no king of France at present', thereby making the point that he had not in fact made a statement, that is, he had not succeeded in saying anything true or false. This amounts to saying that descriptions must be referring expressions because an important part of their contribution to the truth-values of sentences containing them is that, unless they refer, the sentences in question do not have a truth-value at all.

Strawson's use of a notion of 'presupposition' to explain how, on his opposed view, descriptions function in sentences, has prompted much critical debate, and so has his preparedness to allow 'truth-value gaps', that is, absence of truth-value in a meaningful sentence—thus breaching the 'principle of bivalence' which says that every (declarative) sentence must have one or other of the two truth-values 'true' and 'false'. But the main response to his criticism of Russell is undoubtedly to say that the fact upon which his case turns, namely, that we would not say 'that's false' when someone says 'the present king of France is bald', does not mean that the description cannot be treated as making an existential claim. It might be true that we would respond by denying that there is a king of France; after all, merely to say 'that's false' might be misleading, because it could imply something quite different, namely, that there is a hairy king of France. But if we reply 'there is no king of France at present' we have in effect acknowledged that use of the description makes an existential claim—for that is exactly what the denial addresses.

Another objection is that Russell did not see that there are two different uses that can be made of descriptions. Consider the following two cases. First, you see a painting you like, and you say, 'the artist who painted this is a genius'. You do not know who the artist is, but you attribute genius to him. Secondly, the painting is 'Madonna of the Rocks', and you know that Leonardo painted it. In admiration you murmur the same sentence. In the first case the description is used 'attributively', in the second 'referentially'. According to Keith Donnellan, who advanced this criticism, Russell's account concerns only attributive uses. This matters because there are cases where a description can be used successfully to refer to someone even if it does not apply to him—'the man drinking champagne over there is bald' can be used to say something true even if the bald man's glass contains only fizzy water.

A response would be to distinguish between semantic and pragmatic levels of analysis. At the semantic level Russell's account applies, and it makes the sentence 'the man drinking champagne is bald' literally false, because although he is indeed bald, he is drinking water. At the pragmatic level reference has been successfully made, and a truth conveyed, because this kind of use gets the job done. But Russell might argue that since his analysis is aimed at a certain type of *expression* standardly taken to be specifically referential, what he says holds good: questions of use are a further matter.

This response does, however, raise questions about the relation of use and meaning. If use is a large part of meaning, facts about it have to be taken centrally into account in explaining how expressions function. The question of how much weight is to be placed on use is controversial; one view claims that it comes close to exhausting meaning, others reject this claim. Russell's theory demands that we think of the semantics of expressions and their uses as at least separable questions.

For this and other reasons mainly related to the philosophically crucial question of reference—of how language hooks onto the world—Russell's theory of descriptions plays an important role in debates in the philosophy of language. For present purposes it is significant as an example of the analytic technique he applied in his attempts to solve problems in the theory of knowledge and metaphysics, as we shall now see.

Perception and Knowledge

One of the central questions of philosophy is: What is knowledge and how do we get it? John Locke and his successors in the empiricist tradition argued that the foundation of contingent knowledge about the world lies in sensory experience—the use of the five senses, aided when necessary by instruments such as telescopes and the like. With this Russell agrees. But empiricism faces challenge from sceptical arguments aimed at showing that our claims to knowledge might often—perhaps always—be unjustified. There are various reasons for this. We sometimes commit errors in perceiving or reasoning, we sometimes dream without knowing that we are dreaming, we are sometimes deluded because of the effects of fever or alcohol. How, on any occasion of claiming to know something, can we be sure that the claim is not undermined in any of these ways?

In *The Problems of Philosophy* (*PP*) in 1912 Russell made his first systematic attempt to address these questions. 'Is there any knowledge', he asks, 'which is so certain that no reasonable man could doubt it?' He answers in the affirmative; but the certainty, as it turns out, is far from the absolute certainty of proof.

On the basis of straightforward observations about perceptual experience—the fact that, say, a table appears to have different colours, shapes and textures depending upon variations either in the perceiver or in the conditions under which it is perceived—we can see that there is a distinction to be drawn between the appearances of things and what they are like in themselves. How can we be sure that appearance faithfully represents the reality we suppose to lie beyond it? The question might even arise, as the sceptical points about dreams and delusions suggest, whether we can be confident that there are indeed real things 'behind' our sense experiences at all.

To deal with these questions Russell introduces the term 'sense-data' to designate the things immediately known in sensation: particular instances in perceptual awareness of colours, sounds, tastes, smells and textures, each class of data corresponding to one of the five senses. Sense-data are to be distinguished from acts of sensing them: they are what we are immediately aware of in acts of sensing. But they must also, as the considerations of the preceding paragraph show, be distinguished from the things in the world outside us with which we suppose them associated. The crucial question therefore is: What is the relation of sense-data to physical objects?

Russell's response to the sceptic who questions our right to claim knowledge of what lies beyond the veil of sense-data, or even to think that physical objects exist at all, is to say that although sceptical arguments are strictly speaking irrefutable, there is nevertheless 'not the slightest reason' to suppose them true (*PP* 17). His strategy is to collect persuasive considerations in support of this view. First, we can take it that our immediate sense-datum experiences have a 'primitive certainty'. We recognize that when we experience sense-data which we naturally regard as associated with, say, a table, we have not said everything there is to be said about the table. We think, for example, that the table continues to exist when we are out of the room. We can buy the table, put a cloth over it, move it about. We require that different perceivers should be able to perceive the *same* table. All this suggests that a table is something over and above the sense-data that appear to us. But if there were no table out there in the world we should have to formulate a complicated hypothesis about there being as many different seeming-tables as there are perceivers, and explain why nevertheless we all talk as if we are perceiving the same object.

But note that on the sceptical view, as Russell points out, we ought not even to think that there are other perceivers either: after all, if we cannot refute scepticism about objects, how are we to refute scepticism about other minds?

Russell cuts through this difficulty by accepting a version of what is called 'the argument to the best explanation'. It is surely far simpler and more powerful, he argues, to adopt the hypothesis that, first, there really are physical objects existing independently of our sensory experience, and, secondly, that they cause our perceptions and therefore 'correspond' to them in a reliable way. Following Hume, Russell regards belief in this hypothesis as 'instinctive'.

To this, he argues, we can add another kind of knowledge, namely, a priori knowledge of the truths of logic and pure mathematics (and even perhaps the fundamental propositions of ethics). Such knowledge is quite independent of experience, and depends wholly upon the self-evidence of the truths known, such as '1 + 1 = 2' and 'A = A'. When perceptual knowledge and a priori knowledge are conjoined they enable us to acquire general knowledge of the world beyond our immediate experience, because the first kind of knowledge gives us empirical data and the second permits us to draw inferences from it.

These two kinds of knowledge can each be further divided into subkinds, described by Russell as immediate and derivative knowledge respectively. He gives the name 'acquaintance' to immediate knowledge of things. The objects of acquaintance are themselves of two sorts: *particulars*, that is, individual sense-data and—perhaps—ourselves; and *universals*. Universals are of various kinds. They include sensible qualities such as redness and smoothness, spatial and temporal relations such as 'to the left of' and 'before', and certain logical abstractions.

Derivative knowledge of things Russell calls 'knowledge by description', which is general knowledge of facts made possible by combination of and inference from what we are acquainted with. One's knowledge that Everest is the world's highest mountain is an example of descriptive knowledge.

Immediate knowledge of truths Russell calls 'intuitive knowledge', and he describes the truths so known as *self-evident*. These are propositions which are just 'luminously evident, and not capable of being deduced from anything more evident'. For example, we just *see* that '1 + 1 = 2' is true. Among the items of intuitive knowledge are reports of immediate experience; if I simply state what sense-data I am now aware of, I cannot (barring trivial slips of the tongue) be wrong.

Derivative knowledge of truths consists of whatever can be inferred from self-evident truths by self-evident principles of deduction.

41

Despite the appearance of rigour introduced by our possession of a priori knowledge, says Russell, we have to accept that our ordinary general knowledge is only as good as its foundation in the 'best explanation' justification and the instincts which render it plausible. Ordinary knowledge amounts at best, therefore, to 'more or less probable opinion'. But when we note that our probable opinions form a coherent and mutually supportive system—the more coherent and stable the system, the greater the probability of the opinions forming it—we see why we are entitled to repose confidence in them.

An important feature of Russell's theory concerns space, and particularly the distinction between the all-embracing public space assumed by science, and the private spaces in which the sense-data of individual perceivers exist. Private space is built out of the various visual, tactual, and other experiences which a perceiver co-ordinates into a matrix with himself at the centre. But because we do not have acquaintance with the public space of science, its existence and nature is wholly a matter of inference.

Thus Russell's first version of a theory of knowledge and perception, as set out in *PP*. It has a brisk common-sense feel about it on first encounter, but it is far from unproblematic. For example, Russell speaks of 'primitive' knowledge and describes it as intuitive; but he does not offer an account of what such knowledge is, beyond saying that it does not require the support of anything more self-evident than itself. But this definition is hardly adequate, and it is obscured further when he adds that there are two kinds of self-evidence, only one of which is basic. Does this distinction make sense? What is 'self-evidence' anyway? Nor does he consider the possibility that two propositions might contradict each other despite appearing self-evident when considered separately. If this were to happen, which is one to choose, and on what additional principles of self-evidence?

Another criticism levelled at Russell's view is that it makes an important but questionable assumption about the basic nature of sense-experience. This is that sense-data, *qua* sensory minima such as particular colours, smells, or sounds, are simply given in experience, and are its most primitive elements. But in fact sensory experience is not 'thin' and immediate in this way at all. Rather, it is a rich and complex experience of houses, trees, people, cats, and clouds—it is phenomenologically 'thick', and sense-data are only arrived at by a sophisticated process of emptying ordinary perceptual experience of everything it normally means to us. Thus we do not see a rectangle and infer that it is a table; we see a table, and when we come to concentrate upon its shape we see that it is a rectangle.

This criticism is undoubtedly right as far as it goes, but there are ways in which it can be accommodated while still allowing us to describe the purely sensory aspect of experience independently of the usual load of beliefs and theories it carries. Since the whole point is that we are trying to justify possession of those beliefs by showing that perceptual experience entitles us to them, we obviously need an account of our perceptual experience considered purely as such, so that we can evaluate its adequacy to the task. Russell's aim in talking of sense-data is to do just that. Moreover Russell recognized that sense-data are not the immediately perceptually *given*; in writings during the decade after *PP* he points out repeatedly that specifications of sense-data come last in analysis, not first in experience.

Another criticism is that Russell assumes that immediate experience is expressible in propositions which, despite the fact that they describe only what is subjectively 'given', can be used as a basis for knowledge of the world. But how can what seems to apply only to private experience, and carries no reference to what is beyond that experience, be the basis for a theory of knowledge? It does not help to say that Russell also allows a priori knowledge of logical principles which permit inferences from these propositions, for there would be no motivation to draw them unless, in addition, the subject possessed some general empirical beliefs to serve as the major premises in such inferences, and some empirical hypotheses which the inferences in effect test or support. But these are not available to an experiencer possessed only, as Russell presents him, with sense-data and the self-evident truths of logic.

This problem carried weight with Russell himself, and much later (in *Human Knowledge*) he dealt with it by accepting a version of something he otherwise deprecated in the philosophy of Kant, namely, that there have to be some things (other than truths of logic) known to us a priori if knowledge is to be possible at all. This highly important point is discussed in the appropriate place below.

Another problem advanced by critics is that the considerations Russell relies upon to show that there is an appearance–reality distinction do not, as he states them, persuade. The fact that an object looks one colour or shape to one perceiver but another colour or shape to another perceiver, or different colours or shapes to the same perceiver under different conditions—for example, depending upon whether he sees it in daylight or darkness, or from one viewpoint or another—tells us that the question of how objects appear to perception is a complicated matter, but it does not by itself tell us that we are perceiving something other than the object in question.

This criticism is valid as it stands, but it happens that there are other perfectly adequate ways of drawing an appearance–reality distinction, as more recent work in the philosophy of perception shows; so Russell's arguments here can be regarded—as he regarded them himself—as heuristic, that is, as merely illustrating the point in order to get discussion started.

But this criticism suggests a further and more important one. It is that Russell, like all his predecessors since Descartes and like some of his successors such as H. H. Price and A. J. Ayer, accepted a crucially significant assumption from Descartes. This is that the right starting-point for an enquiry into knowledge is individual experience. The individual is to begin with the private data of consciousness, and find reasons among them to support his inferences to—or, more generally, beliefs about—a world outside his head. One of the major shifts in twentieth-century philosophy has been the rejection of this Cartesian assumption. Among the serious difficulties with this assumption is that scepticism becomes impossible either to ignore or refute if we accept it. Another is that on such a thin basis we are simply not entitled to think of the solipsistic would-be knower, alone inside his mind, as capable of naming and thinking about his sensations and experiences, still less as being able to reason from them to an external world. Both thoughts push us firmly towards the thought that the proper place to begin epistemology is, somehow, in the public domain.

The External World and Other Minds

Russell himself was not content with the way he had set out matters in *PP*, which after all was intended as a popular book and did not offer a rigorous exposition of its theses. Over the next four decades he returned to the problem of knowledge and perception repeatedly. In the years between publication of *PP* and the outbreak of the First World War he devoted himself seriously to them, drafting his big *Theory of Knowledge* manuscript, part of which he published and part of which he abandoned, and writing a major series of lectures which appeared in 1914 as *Our Knowledge of the External World* (*OKEW*). In this work he gives more detailed thought to aspects of the theory in *PP*, with significant results.

One difference between the theories of *PP* and *OKEW* is that Russell had come to see that the experiencing subject's basis for knowledge—the sense-data that appear to him alone, and his intuitive knowledge of the laws of logic—is too slender a starting-point. He was not rejecting the Cartesian assumption just discussed; rather, now somewhat more sensitive to the difficulties it poses, he was trying to limit them. He accordingly places greater weight on the subject's possessing facts of memory, and a grasp of spatial and temporal relations holding among the elements of a current experience. The subject is also empowered to compare data, for example as to differences of colour and shape. Ordinary common beliefs, and belief in the existence of other minds, are still excluded.

With this enriched basis of what he now calls 'hard data', Russell formulates the question to be answered thus: 'can the existence of anything other than our own hard data be inferred?' His approach is first to show how we can construct, as a hypothesis, a notion of space into which the facts of experience—both the subject's own and those he learns by the testimony of others—can be placed. Then, to see whether we have reason for believing that this spatial world is real, Russell gives an argument for believing that other minds exist, because if one is indeed entitled to believe this, then one can rely on the testimony of others, which, jointly with one's own experience, will give powerful support to the view that there is a spatial—that is, a real—world.

This strategy is ingenious. In the paper 'The Relation of Sense-Data to Physics', written in early 1914, Russell adds to it an equally ingenious way of thinking about the relation of sense-experience to things. In *PP* he had said that we infer the existence of physical things from our sense-data; now he describes them as functions of sense-data, or as he sometimes puts it, 'constructions' out of sense-data. This employs the technique of logic in which one thing can be shown to be analysable into things of another kind. Russell describes as the 'supreme maxim of scientific philosophising' the principle that 'wherever possible, logical constructions are to be substituted for inferred entities'. In accordance with this principle, physical objects are accordingly to be analysed as constructions out of sense-data; yet not out of actual or occurrent sense-data only, but out of 'sensibilia' also, by which is meant 'appearances' or, in Russell's phrase, 'how things appear', irrespective of whether they constitute sense-data which are currently part of any perceiver's experience. This is intended to explain what it is for an object to exist when not being perceived.

An important aspect of this view is, Russell now holds, that sense-data and sensibilia are not private mental entities, but part of the actual subject-matter of physics. They are indeed 'the ultimate constituents of the physical world', because it is in terms of them that verification of common sense and physics ultimately depends. This is important because we usually think that sense-data are functions of physical objects, that is, exist and have their nature because physical objects cause them; but verification is only possible if matters are the other way round, with physical objects as functions of sense-data. This theory 'constructs' physical objects out of sensibilia; the existence of these latter therefore verifies the existence of the former.

Instead of developing this distinctive theory further, Russell abandoned it; in later work, particularly in *The Analysis of Matter* (*AMt*) in 1927 and *Human Knowledge* (*HK*) in 1948, he reverted to treating physical objects, and the space they occupy, as inferred from sense-experience. A number of considerations made him do this. One was his acceptance, driven by the sciences of physics and human physiology, of the standard view they offer that perception is caused by the action of the physical environment on our sense organs. 'Whoever accepts the causal theory of perception', he writes, 'is compelled to conclude that percepts are in our heads, for they come at the end of a causal chain of physical events leading, spatially, from the object to the brain of the percipient' (*AMt* 32). He also, in *The Analysis of Mind* (*AMd*) in 1921 gave up talk of 'sense-data', and ceased to distinguish between the act of sensing and what is sensed. His reason for this relates to his theory of the mind, sketched later.

Another major reason for Russell's abandonment of the theory was the sheer complexity and, as he came to see it, implausibility of the views he tried to formulate about private and public spaces, the relations between them, and the way sensibilia are supposed to occupy them. He makes a passing mention of this cluster of problems in *MPD*. And he there reports that his main reason for abandoning 'the attempt to construct "matter" out of experienced data alone' is that it 'is an impossible programme . . . physical objects cannot be interpreted as structures composed of elements actually experienced' (*MPD* 79). Now, this last remark is not strictly consistent with Russell's stated view in the original texts that sensibilia do not have to be actually sensed; *MPD* gives a much more phenomenalistic gloss to the theory than its original statement does. But it touches upon a serious problem with the theory: which is that it seems simply incoherent to speak of an 'unsensed sense-datum' that does not even require—as its very name seems *per contra* to demand—an essential connection with perception.

Giving up the project embodied in the *Theory of Knowledge* manuscript and *OKEW* was doubtless a blow to Russell, because when, after finishing *PM*, he turned his attention to questions of knowledge and perception, he saw the task of solving problems about the relation between these matters and physics as his next major contribution. It was an ambition he had nourished since the late 1890s.

There are other important questions in epistemology to which, in these endeavours, Russell gave only passing attention. They concern the kind of reasoning traditionally supposed to be the mainstay of science, namely, non-demonstrative inference. It was some years before Russell returned to consider these questions: the main discussion he gives is to be found in *HK*, written after the Second World War. In the meantime he turned his attention to certain questions of method and metaphysics which, during the course of his work on perception, had come to seem to him important. These questions are the subject of the next chapter.

3 Philosophy, Mind, and Science

Method and Metaphysics

Russell gave the name 'logical atomism' to the views he developed
from *OKEW* onwards. Logical atomism is principally a method,
and Russell hoped that it would resolve questions about the nature
of perception and its relation to physics. It is important to note
that Russell's philosophical work in the four decades after *Principia
Mathematica* is chiefly devoted to the particular question of the
relation of perception to physics, and is in effect thus an attempt to provide a (qualified) empirical basis for science, considered
as the theory of the world which has the best chance of being true
or at least on the way to truth. Logical atomism also thereby gave
Russell his metaphysics—that is, his account of the nature of
reality—which turns out not to be, at least in a straightforward
way, the current physics of matter, but a representation of it as
a logical structure. Russell's accounts of his metaphysical views
almost invariably take the form of a sketch occupying the con-
cluding parts of his various discussions of logical analysis; most
of his attention is devoted to describing the analytical strategy
itself.

The Philosophy of Logical Atomism

Russell describes logical atomism in a number of places, the most
important being the chapter in *OKEW* entitled 'Logic as the
Essence of Philosophy', and the series of lectures delivered in 1918
under the heading 'The Philosophy of Logical Atomism' (reprinted
in Marsh, *Logic and Knowledge*). There is a summary of logical
atomism's methods and aims in the essay 'Logical Atomism' (1924)
also reprinted in Marsh.

A key to the method of logical atomism lies in Russell's claim
that 'logic is the essence of philosophy', where 'logic' means
mathematical logic. Its importance is that it provides the means
of effecting powerful and philosophically revealing analyses of

structures; in particular, the related structures of propositions and facts.

It has already been seen how the analysis of propositions shows that it is a mistake to treat them all as subject-predicate in form, and that in this and related ways surface grammar misleads, as when we take descriptions and ordinary names to be denoting expressions. There is likewise a structure-revealing analysis to be given of the world we talk about when we assert these propositions, and of the propositions themselves.

In 'Logic as the Essence of Philosophy' Russell sketches these two related structures by starting with the former. The world, he says, consists of many things with many qualities and relations. An inventory of the world would require not just a list of things, but of things with these qualities and relations—in other words, it would be an inventory of facts. Things, qualities, and relations are the constituents of facts, and facts can in turn be analysed into them. Facts are expressed by what Russell calls 'propositions', defined as 'forms of words asserted as true or false'. Propositions which express basic facts—that is, which simply assert that a thing has a certain quality or stands to some other thing in a certain relation—he calls 'atomic propositions'. When these are combined by means of logical words such as 'and', 'or', and 'if–then', the result is complex or 'molecular' propositions. Such propositions are exceedingly important because all possibility of inference depends upon them.

Finally there are 'general propositions' such as 'all men are mortal' (and their denials, formed with the word 'some' as in 'some men are not mortal'). The facts they express depend to some degree upon a priori knowledge. This crucial point emerges as a result of reflection upon the analysis of propositions and facts. Theoretically, if we knew all the atomic facts, and that they are *all* the atomic facts, we could infer all other truths from them. But general propositions cannot be known by inference from atomic facts alone. Consider 'all men are mortal': if we knew each individual man and his mortality, we still could not infer that all men are mortal until we knew that these were all the men there are; and this is a general proposition. Russell was keen to stress the importance of this point. Because general truths cannot be inferred from particular truths alone, and because all empirical evidence is of particular truths, it follows that there must be some general a priori knowledge if there is knowledge at all. Russell took this to refute the older empiricists, for whom all knowledge rests solely on sense experience.

The question immediately arises as to where such general knowledge is found. Russell's answer remains what it had been in *PP*: such knowledge is found in logic, which provides us with completely general self-evident propositions. Consider the proposition, 'all men are mortal, Socrates is a man, therefore Socrates is mortal'. It contains empirical terms ('Socrates', 'man', 'mortal') and is therefore not a proposition of pure logic. But the proposition of pure logic which represents its form, 'if anything has a certain property, and whatever has this property has a certain other property, then this thing has this other property' (clearer still: 'all Fs are Gs, x is F, therefore x is G') is both completely general and self-evident. Just such propositions take us beyond the limits of empirical particularity.

In 'The Philosophy of Logical Atomism' the details of this analytical programme are spelled out in greater detail. The 'logical' in the label signals that the atoms are arrived at as the 'last residue of analysis' where the analysis is logical rather than physical (PLA 178). They are particulars such as 'little patches of colour or sounds, momentary things—and . . . predicates or relations'. The aim is to pass from ordinary beliefs about the world to an accurate grasp of how experience underwrites science; that is, to pass from 'those obvious, vague, ambiguous things, that we feel quite sure of, to something precise, clear, definite, which by reflection and analysis we find is involved in the vague thing we start from, and is, so to speak, the real truth of which that vague thing is a sort of shadow' (ibid.). The method is analysis of complex symbols—propositions—into the simple symbols from which they are combined; the terminus of such analysis is 'direct acquaintance with the objects which are the meanings of [the] simple symbols' where 'meaning' means 'denotation' (PLA 194). In a 'logically perfect language' such as *Principia Mathematica* is intended to provide, the components of a proposition—the simple symbols—correspond one-to-one with the components of a fact, except for the logical expressions 'or', 'and', and the like. Each simple object is denoted by its own different simple symbol. Such a language, says Russell, shows 'at a glance the logical structure of the facts asserted or denied' (PLA 198).

On this basis Russell offers an 'excursus into metaphysics'. Logical atomism is the view that in theory, if not in practice, analysis takes us down to the ultimate simples out of which the world is built. Simples are defined as whatever is non-complex—that is, not further analysable—and each is an independent self-subsisting thing. They are, moreover, very short-lived, so the complexes built out of them are 'logical fictions', put together to serve our epistemic and practical purposes.

Simples come in infinitely many kinds. There are various orders of particulars, qualities, and relations, but their common feature is that they have a reality not shared by anything else. The only other objects in the world are facts, which are the things that get asserted or denied by propositions. Facts do not have the same reality as their constituents, and knowledge of them is quite different from knowledge of simples; the former is knowledge by description, the latter knowledge by acquaintance.

Russell's method of analysis involves Ockham's Razor, the principle that we should work with the most economical theory possible about what exists. It can be described as posing an insistent question, 'What is the smallest number of simple undefined things at the start, and the smallest number of undemonstrated premisses, out of which you can define the things that need to be defined and prove the things that need to be proved?' (PLA 271). When Ockham's Razor is applied, the account to be given of an ordinary physical object, such as a desk, is as follows. We think of the desk as an enduring object which exists when unperceived. As a sceptic might point out, this belief is based on intermittent perceptions of the desk, which by themselves tell us nothing about whether the desk continues to exist between times. Yet we say that all these different appearances of the desk are appearances of the *same* desk. What makes us say this? Russell's answer is that the series of appearances is simply defined by us into a single persisting object. 'In that way the desk is reduced to being a logical fiction, because a series is a logical fiction. In that way all the ordinary objects of daily life are extruded from the world of what there is, and in their place as what there is you find a number of passing particulars of the kind that one is immediately conscious of in sense,' namely, sense-data (PLA 273). So the things we call real things 'are systems, series of classes of particulars, and the particulars are the real things, the particulars being sense-data when they happen to be given to you' (PLA 274).

This way with matters suggested to Russell an analysis of physics—physical atoms are construed as logical fictions too—and it began to incline him towards a view of mind called 'neutral monism'. He did not work out either view fully at this stage; but later, and on the basis of some important changes in his outlook, he gave them express attention. He did so in *The Analysis of Matter* (1927) and *The Analysis of Mind* (1921) respectively. I defer more particular discussion of them to pp. 57–64 below.

Some Problems in Logical Atomism

It is difficult to find logical atomism satisfactory. For one thing, Russell's presentation of it is sketchy, and yet it is aimed at solving many different problems at once. It is an empiricist theory of meaning, which means that it has to offer component theories of knowledge, perception, and mind, with, at their centre, an empiricist account of how words work, and of how they are learned and understood. This latter task is complicated for Russell by his view that the surface forms of ordinary language are misleading and therefore, if not correctly analysed, will lead to bad philosophy:

I think the importance of philosophical grammar is very much greater than it is generally thought to be. I think that practically all traditional metaphysics is filled with mistakes due to bad grammar, and that almost all the traditional problems of metaphysics and traditional results— supposed results—of metaphysics are due to a failure to make the kind of distinctions in what we may call philosophical grammar. (PLA 269)

So the analysis proceeds by assuming that there is an underlying structure of language, importantly different from its surface structure, which alone corresponds to the structure of the world revealed by its analysis. One large problem this therefore raises is whether the logic of *Principia Mathematica* is uniquely the correct way to represent the underlying logical form of natural language.

Russell's theory unites a purely logical account of structure to a sense-data empiricism, by making sense-data the simples constituting the world's structure. But it is necessary for him to include among simples not just things but their qualities and relations—that is, universals—and this immediately introduces another difficulty, for it is not clear that universals are simple in the way particulars are supposed to be. The marks of simplicity are unanalysability and independence. Do universals have these marks, even in Russell's best example of colour-patches of a specific shade? No; for colour-patches are not independent of one another, and the expressions denoting them are capable of introducing incompatibilities between propositions.

Russell believed that such problems could be overcome by a completely thorough analysis of ordinary factual discourse. But he was never able to carry out such an analysis, and had to regard it as something for future scientific philosophy to achieve—or to deal with differently, if it could discover a way. This led him to make some interesting admissions:

When I speak of simples, I ought to explain that I am speaking of something not experienced as such, but known only inferentially as the limit of analysis. It is quite possible that, by greater logical skill, the need for assuming them could be avoided. A logical language will not lead to error if its simple symbols (i.e. those not having any parts that are symbols, or any significant structure) all stand for objects of some one type, even if these objects are not simple. The only drawback to such a language is that it is incapable of dealing with anything simpler than the objects which it represents by simple symbols. But I confess it seems obvious to me (as it did to Leibniz) that what is complex must be composed of simples, though the number of constituents may be infinite. (*Logic and Knowledge*, 337)

In this passage Russell effectively concedes the problem of attaching his empiricism to his atomism—if sense-data are simples, and yet simples are inferred not experienced, then the theory is incoherent—and breaks the connection, elsewhere insisted upon, between simple symbols and simple entities: for here he is saying that simple symbols can stand for complex entities; the only requirement is that they should be of one type. Moreover, if simples are infinite in number the prospects even for a logically *perfect* language are exceedingly dim, because it would have to contain an infinity of names, and analysis itself, as a potentially infinite procedure, would never be fully achievable.

Some commentators suggest that logical atomism would fare

better if it were detached from empiricism and treated as a purely formal theory, as Wittgenstein treated it in the *Tractatus Logico-Philosophicus*. So considered, its essence is that expressions (other than those of logic, such as 'and') are of two kinds, those that denote existing (simple) things and those that are analysable into such expressions. When we leave aside the empiricism which says that the simple things are sense-data and therefore objects of acquaintance, we thereby leave aside any account of how people can learn and understand language, and this is a serious defect; it certainly mattered to Russell that such an account should be available, and it marks one of the chief differences between his and Wittgenstein's versions of atomism. But since, as noted, trying to graft empiricism to atomism creates such difficulties, this defect might have to be accepted—although it would be entirely natural to argue that the incompatibility of atomism with these considerations (treated as constraints on any adequate account of language) might instead be taken as a reason for abandoning atomism itself.

But trying to detach empiricism from atomism makes difficulties for, among other things, Russell's theory of names. According to this theory, logically proper names are very like the demonstratives 'this' and 'that'; they are empty of descriptive content, and their meanings are the particulars they denote. These meanings can therefore only be learned in episodes of acquaintance with the particulars they denote; but detaching empirical considerations means that this part of the theory is not now available. This creates a problem; for one of the main applications of this view lies in analysis of ordinary language expressions which appear to denote temporally persisting things—desks and the like. The pure form of the theory requires that, for each logically proper name, something exists for it to denote. On the empiricist theory such denotata are momentary sense-data, and therefore in addition to knowing what names denote, we know that they share an aspect of their denotata; they are temporary also. But on the pure theory it is not clear how to characterize names, because we do not know what the unknown—purely formal—ultimate existents are. Denying ourselves a theory about this means further that we have no view of how the naming relation works; there is, for example, no baptismal occasion as when, on the empiricist theory, someone christens a given sense-datum 'that' or something equally suitable. And this also means that we have nothing to say about why *this* name names *that* particular, and whether it could have named another; which anyway might seem a small problem once we have allowed ourselves to think of there being names without namers, language-learners, or perceivers.

This cluster of considerations suggests that the gain to be had from detaching atomism and empiricism is severely limited. It happens that these objections are not by themselves fatal to those aspects of logical atomism which offer an account of meaning; there are other ways of developing them, along with their connections to language-understanding. But a full evaluation should anyway take account of Russell's own reasons for modifying some and abandoning other—rather central—features of logical atomism in his later thinking about mind and matter. To a sketch of these points I now turn.

Mind and Matter

In the course of setting out his logical atomist views in 1918 Russell said that he was tempted but still unconvinced by William James's 'neutral monism', a theory offered to solve long-standing problems about the differences and connections between mind and matter. Summarily stated, James's theory is that the world ultimately consists neither of mental stuff, as idealists hold, nor material stuff, as materialists hold, but of a 'neutral stuff' from which the appearance of both mind and matter is formed. By Russell's own account, he was converted to this theory soon after finishing the lectures on logical atomism. He had written about James's views in 1914, and rejected them; in the 1918 lectures he was more sympathetic, but still undecided; but finally in a paper entitled 'On Propositions' (1919) he embraced the theory, and used it as a basis in 1921 for his book *The Analysis of Mind* (*AMd*). Russell refined the theory somewhat thereafter, but I shall draw mainly on *AMd* for this sketch.

Popular philosophy has it that mind and matter are very different, and that the difference lies in the fact that minds are conscious whereas material things, such as stones, are not. The question Russell therefore asks is: Is consciousness the essence of the mental? To answer this, one needs first to have some idea of the nature of consciousness. Reflection on standard examples of conscious phenomena—perceiving, remembering, thinking, believing—suggests that the principal feature of consciousness is that *to be conscious* in any of these ways is *to be conscious of* something. Philosophers give the name 'intentionality' to this characteristic, which might also be labelled 'aboutness' or 'directedness'. Thus the notion of consciousness is an essentially relational one; an *act* of mind—an act of perceiving, or believing, or some such—is related to an *object*—the object perceived, the proposition believed. Indeed on some versions of the theory, for example Meinong's, there are three elements in play: the act, the content, and the object. For example: suppose one thinks of St Paul's Cathedral in London. There is one's act of thinking; there is the character of the thought that makes it about St Paul's and not about some other cathedral—this is the content; and then there is the object, namely, St Paul's itself.

Russell rejects such views. First, he says, there is no such thing as the 'act'. The occurrence of the content of a thought is the occurrence of the thought, and there is neither empirical evidence nor theoretical need for an 'act' in addition. Russell's diagnosis of why anyone might think otherwise is that we say, 'I think so-and-so', which suggests that thinking is an act performed by a subject. But he rejects this, for reasons very similar to those advanced by Hume, who held that the notion of the self is a fiction, and that we are empirically licensed to say no more than that there are bundles of thoughts which for convenience we parcel as 'me' and 'you'.

Secondly, Russell criticizes the relation of content and object. Meinong and others had taken it that the relation is one of direct reference, but in Russell's view it is more complicated and derivative, consisting largely of beliefs about a variety of more and less indirect connections among contents, between contents and objects, and among objects. Add to this the fact that, in imagination and non-standard experiences like hallucination, one can have thoughts without objects, and one sees that the content–object relation involves many difficulties—not least, Russell says, in giving rise to the dispute between idealists who think that content is more significant than objects, and realists who think objects are more significant than content. (Russell's use of these labels, although standard, is misleading: we should for accuracy substitute the label 'anti-realist' for 'idealist' here; this is because whereas, at bottom, realism and anti-realism are indeed differing theses about the relation of contents to objects, and thus are *epistemological* theses, idealism is a *metaphysical* thesis about the nature of the world, namely, that it is ultimately mental in character. This point is frequently missed in philosophical debate, so Russell is in good company.) All these difficulties can be avoided, Russell claims, if we adopt a version of William James's 'neutral monist' theory.

Neutral Monism

James argued that the single kind of metaphysically ultimate raw material is arranged in different patterns by its interrelations, some of which we call 'mental' and some 'physical'. James said his view was prompted by dissatisfaction with theories of consciousness, which is merely the wispy inheritor of old-fashioned talk about 'souls'. He agreed that thoughts exist; what he denied is that they are entities. They are, instead, functions: there is 'no aboriginal stuff or quality of being, contrasted with that of which material objects are made, out of which our thoughts of them are made; but there is a function in experience which thoughts perform, and for the performance of which this quality of being is invoked. That function is *knowing*' (James, *Essays in Radical Empiricism*, 3–4).

In James's view the single kind of 'primal stuff', as he called it, is 'pure experience'. Knowing is a relation into which different portions of primal stuff can enter; the relation itself is as much part of pure experience as its relata.

Russell could not accept quite all of this view. He thought that James's use of the phrase 'pure experience' showed a lingering influence of idealism, and rejected it; he preferred the use made by others of the term 'neutral stuff', a nomenclatural move of importance because whatever the primal stuff is, it has to be able—when differently arranged—to give rise to what could not appropriately be called 'experience', for example stars and stones. But even with this modified view Russell only partially agreed. It is right to reject the idea of consciousness as an entity, he said, and it is partly but not wholly right to consider both mind and matter as composed of neutral stuff which in isolation is neither; especially in regard to sensations—an important point for Russell, with his overriding objective of marrying physics and perception. But he insisted that certain things belong only to the mental world (images and feelings) and others only to the physical world (everything which cannot be described as experience). What distinguishes them is the kind of causality that governs them; there are two different kinds of causal law, one applicable only to psychological phenomena, the other only to physical phenomena. Hume's law of association exemplifies the first kind, the law of gravity the second. Sensation obeys both kinds, and is therefore truly neutral.

Adopting this version of neutral monism obliged Russell to abandon some of his earlier views. One important change was that he gave up the notion of 'sense-data'. He did this because sense-data are objects of mental acts, whose existence he had now rejected; therefore, since there can be no question of a relation between non-existent acts and supposed objects of those acts, there can be no such objects either. And because there is no distinction between sensation and sense-datum—that is, because we now understand that the sensation we have in seeing, for example, a colour-patch *just is* the colour-patch itself—we need only one term here, for which Russell adopts the name 'percept'.

Before accepting neutral monism Russell had objected to it on a number of grounds, one being that it could not properly account for belief. And as noted, even when he adopted the theory he did so in a qualified form; mind and matter overlap on common ground, but each has irreducible aspects. Nevertheless what at last persuaded him was the fact, as it seemed to him, that psychology and physics had come very close: the new physics both of the atom and of relativistic space–time had effectively dematerialized matter, and psychology, especially in the form of behaviourism, had effectively materialized mind. From the internal viewpoint of introspection, mental reality is composed of sensations and images. From the external viewpoint of observation, material things are composed of sensations and sensibilia. A more or less unified theory therefore seems possible by treating the fundamental difference as one of arrangement: a mind is a construction formed of materials organized in one way, a brain more or less the same materials organized in another.

A striking feature of this view is, surprisingly, how idealist it is. Russell had, as noted, charged James with residual idealism. But here he is arguing something hardly distinguishable: that minds are composed of sensed percepts—namely, sensations and images— and matter is a logical fiction constructed of unsensed percepts. Now Russell had often insisted (using his earlier terminology) that sense-data and sensibilia are 'physical' entities, in somewhat the sense in which, if one were talking about an item of sensory information in a nervous system, that datum would be present as impulses in a nerve or activity in a brain. But then nerves and brains, as objects of physical theory, are themselves to be under- stood as constructions from sensations and sensibilia, not as tra- ditionally understood 'material substance', a concept which physics has shown to be untenable. At the end of *AMd* Russell accord- ingly says that 'an ultimate scientific account of what goes on in the world, if it were ascertainable, would resemble psychology rather than physics . . . [because] psychology is nearer to what exists' (*AMd* 305, 308). This explains Russell's notorious claim that 'brains consist of thoughts' and that when a physiologist looks at another person's brain, what he 'sees' is a portion of his own brain (Schilpp, *Philosophy of Bertrand Russell*, 705).

For robuster versions of materialism this aspect of Russell's view is hard to accept. But it is not the only difficulty with his version of neutral monism. Not least is the fact that he failed in his main aim, which was to refute the view that consciousness is essential to the distinction between mental and physical phenom- ena. He had not of course attempted to analyse consciousness quite away; his aim was rather to reduce its importance for the mind–matter question. But images, feelings, and sensations, which play so central a role in his theory, stubbornly remain *conscious* phenomena, whereas the sensibilia (by definition often unsensed), which constitute the greater part of matter, are not. Russell ac- cepted this, but tried to specify a criterion of difference which did not trade on these facts, namely, the criterion of membership of different causal realms. But whereas that difference is open to question—and even if it exists might be too often hard to see—the consciousness difference is clear cut.

Relatedly, the intentionality which characterizes consciousness cannot be left out of accounts of knowledge; memory and perception are inexplicable without it. Russell later acknowledged this point, and gave it as a reason in *MPD* for having to return to the question of perception and knowledge in later writings.

Russell also later came to abandon the idea—anyway deeply unsatisfactory from the point of view of a theory supposed to be both *neutral* and *monist*—that images and feelings are essentially mental, that is, not wholly reducible to neutral stuff; for in a very late essay he says, 'An event is not rendered either mental or material by any intrinsic quality, but only by its causal relations. It is perfectly possible for an event to have both the causal relations characteristic of physics and those characteristic of psychology. In that case, the event is both mental and material at once' (*Portraits from Memory* (1958), 152). This, for consistency, is what he should have argued in *AMd* itself, where only sensations have this character. But this view in turn generates another problem, which is that it comes into unstable tension with a view to which Russell returned after *AMd*, namely, that the causes of percepts are inferred from the occurrence of the percepts themselves. As noted earlier, Russell wavered between treating physical things as logical constructions of sensibilia and as entities inferred as the causes of perception; he held this latter view in *PP* and returned to it after *AMd*. But on the face of it, one is going to need a delicate connection between one's metaphysics and one's epistemology in order to hold both that minds and things are of one stuff, and that things are the unknown external inferred causes of what happens in minds. So those parts of the legacy of *AMd* which remain in his later thinking raise considerable difficulties for his later views about matter.

Realism and Perception

One of the chief reasons for Russell's reversion to a realistic, inferential view about physical things was the difficulty inherent in the notion of unsensed sense-data or, in the later terminology, percepts. As noted above, the idea had been to replace inferred entities with logically constructed ones, an application of the analytical technique. If physical things can be logically constructed

out of actual and possible sense-data, then two desiderata have
been realized at once: the theory is empirically based, and inferred
entities have been shaved away by Ockham's Razor. But it is obvious, and the point has already been made, that the idea of unsensed
sense-data (or unperceived percepts) is, if not indeed contradictory, at least problematic. It makes sense—although, without a
careful gloss, it is metaphysically questionable—to talk of the
existence of *possibilities* of sensation; but to talk of the existence
of *possible sensations* arguably does not (note Russell's definition
of sensibilia as entities having the 'same metaphysical and physical status as sense-data without necessarily being data to any
mind'). If the choice lay between inferred material particulars and
non-actual perceptions existing unperceived, it would seem best
to plump for the former. In effect, this is what Russell himself
came to think; and unsensed sensations went out of the window.
But he did not return to the cruder form of inferential realism
held in *PP*; something more ingenious, but no more successful,
was up his sleeve, as explained shortly.

Another reason for Russell's reversion to realism was his recog-
nition that the notion of causality is problematic for phenomenalism. Things in the world seem to affect one another causally in
ways that are difficult to account for properly by mere reports of
sense-experiences. Moreover a causal theory of perception is a
natural and powerful way of explaining how experience itself arises.
In Russell's mature philosophy of science, contained in *AMt* and
Human Knowledge (1948), he did not opt for a Lockean view
which says that our percepts resemble their causal origins—the
so-called 'picture-original' theory—because we cannot be directly
acquainted with things, and therefore cannot expect to know their
qualities and relations. Rather, he now argued, changes in the
world and our perceptions are correlated, or co-vary, at least for
orders of things in the world that our perceptual apparatus is
competent to register (we do not, for example, perceive electrons
swarming in the table, so there is no associated covariation of
world and perception at that level). The correspondence between
percepts and things is one of *structure* at the appropriate level:
'Whatever we infer from perceptions it is only structure that we
can validly infer; and structure is what can be expressed by mathematical logic' (*AMt* 254). And this means that we have to be

'agnostic' about all but the physical world's mathematical properties, which is what physics describes (*AMt* 270).

Russell had come to think that the best candidate for what is metaphysically most basic in the world is the 'event'. Objects are constructed out of events in the following way: the world is a collection of events, most of which cluster together around a multitude of 'centres', thus constituting individual 'objects'. Each cluster radiates 'chains' of events, which interact with and react upon chains radiating from other centres—among which are perceivers. When a chain interacts with the events constituting the perceptual apparatus of a perceiver, the last link in the chain is a percept. Since everything is ultimately constituted of events, they are in effect the 'neutral stuff' of which minds and material things are made. Minds are clusters of events connected by 'mental' relations, not least among them memory; otherwise there is no metaphysical difference between mind and matter. Finally, the interrelations of event-chains is what scientific causal laws describe.

This view enabled Russell to formulate the argument he had long been trying to state satisfactorily, namely, that percepts are parts of things. For on this view it is not the case that there are events which constitute things, and then in addition other events which are perceptions of those things; rather, there are just events constituting the object, some of which are percepts—these being the terminal events of the chains radiating from the object which interact with events constituting the perceiver.

This theory is inferential not in the earlier sense in which the causes of percepts, lying inaccessibly beyond a veil of perception, are guessed from the nature of the percepts themselves. Rather, the inference is *from* certain terminal events, namely, percepts—which are interactions between (to put the matter heuristically) 'mental' events and that level of structure in the rest of the event-world with which the 'mental' events are capable of interacting—*to* the clusters and chains of events constituting the world as a whole.

In *AMt* the core of the theory is the idea that knowledge of the world is purely structural. We know the qualities and relations as well as the structure of percepts, but we know only the structure of external events, not their qualities. This seems somewhat reminiscent of Locke's distinction between primary and second-ary qualities, but it is not; Russell is saying that all we can infer from our percepts is the structure of the qualities and relations of things, not the qualities and relations themselves; and that this is the limit of knowledge.

This theory has a fatal flaw, which was quickly recognized by the mathematician M. H. A. Newman and set out in an article published soon after the appearance of *AMt*. It is that since our knowledge of the structure of events is not a mere result of our stipulating them, but is manifestly non-trivial, it follows that our inferential knowledge cannot be limited solely to questions of structure. This is because—to put the point by a rough analogy—a number of different worlds could be abstractly definable as hav-ing the same structure, and if they were, knowledge of their struc-ture alone could not separate them and in particular could not individuate the 'real' one. If science genuinely consists of discov-eries about the world through observation and experiment, the distinction between what we observe and what we infer cannot therefore be collapsed into a distinction between pure structure and qualities.

Russell wrote a characteristically generous letter to Newman acknowledging the point: 'You make it entirely obvious that my statements to the effect that nothing is known about the physical world except its structure are either false or trivial, and I am somewhat ashamed not to have noticed it myself.'

Familiarly by now, the common thread linking Russell's earlier and later views was his desire to reconcile science and perception, with the particular aim of basing the former on the relative cer-tainty of the latter and thus furnishing it with grounds. He saw the chief problem in any such enterprise as securing the move from perception to the objects of physical theory. On his view, this move must either be inferential, in which it takes us from the incorrigible data of sense to something else, or it is analytic, that is, consists in a process of constructing physical entities out of percepts. On the later view just reported, the inference has a special advantage over more usual inferential theories, in that the inference is not from one kind of thing to another, but from one part of something to its other parts.

In his earlier views Russell had accorded primary reality to sense-data and built everything else out of them. On the later view, reality belongs to events as the ultimate entities, and an important change of emphasis is introduced: percepts remain immediate and as certain as anything can be, but they are not construed as having accurately to represent the physical world, which, in the picture offered by science as the most powerful way to understand it, is anyway very different from how it appears.

Inference and Science

Crucially, however, there remains a familiar and major problem about whether inferences from perception to the world are secure. A large part of Russell's aim in *Human Knowledge* (*HK*) was to state grounds for taking them to be so. Throughout his thinking about the relation of perception and science he was convinced that something has to be known a priori for scientific knowledge to be possible. Earlier, as noted, he thought that purely logical principles provide such knowledge. But he now saw that logic alone is insufficient; we must know something more substantial. His solution was to say that inference from perception to events is justified in the light of certain a priori 'postulates' which nevertheless state contingent facts about the word. So stated, Russell's view immediately reminds one of Kant's thesis that possession of 'synthetic a priori knowledge' is a condition of the possibility of knowledge in general, a view which Russell robustly dismisses in the Preface to *HK*. The difference is explained by the tentative and probabilistic account that Russell, in this last major attempt to state a theory of knowledge, felt was all that could be hoped for.

Two features of Russell's approach in *HK* explain this result. One is that he now thought that knowledge should be understood in 'naturalistic' terms, that is, as a feature of our biological circumstances, taken together with the way the world is constituted. The other is that he had come to make a virtue of the fact that the basic data of knowledge are never certain, but at best merely credible to some degree. This second point enters into the detailed working out of the views in *HK*. The first makes its appearance whenever Russell needs to justify the justifications that *HK* attempts to provide for scientific knowledge.

When data have a certain credibility independently of their relations to other data, Russell describes them as having a degree of 'intrinsic' credibility. Propositions having some intrinsic credibility lend support to propositions inferred from them. The chief question then becomes: How do propositions with some measure of intrinsic credibility transfer that credibility to the hypotheses of science? Another way of framing the question is to ask how reports of observation and experiment can function as evidence. This is where Russell's postulates come in.

There are five postulates. The first, 'the postulate of quasi-permanence', is intended to replace the ordinary idea of a persisting thing: 'given any event A, it happens very frequently that, at any neighbouring time, there is at some neighbouring place an event very similar to A'. Thus the objects of common sense are analysed into sequences of similar events. The ancestor of this idea is Hume's analysis of the 'identity' of things in terms of our propensity to take a sequence of resembling perceptions to be evidence for a single thing, as when you have perceptions of a rose bush every time you go into the garden, and therefore take it that there is a single persisting rose bush there even when no perceivers are present.

The second, 'the postulate of separable causal lines', states that 'it is frequently possible to form a series of events such that, from one or two members of the series, something can be inferred as to all the other members'. For example, we can keep track of a billiard ball throughout a game of billiards; common sense thinks of the ball as a single thing changing its position, which according to this postulate is to be explained by treating the ball and its movements as a series of events from some of which you can infer information about the others.

The third is 'the postulate of spatio-temporal continuity', designed to deny 'action at a distance' by requiring that if there is a causal connection between two events that are not contiguous, there must be a chain of intermediate links between them. Many of our inferences to unobserved occurrences depend upon this postulate.

The fourth is 'the structural postulate', which states that 'when a number of structurally similar complexes are ranged about a centre in regions not widely separated, it is usually the case that all belong to causal lines having their origin in an event of the same structure at the centre'. This is intended to make sense of the idea that there exists a world of physical objects common to all perceivers. If six million people all listen to the Prime Minister's broadcast on the wireless, and upon comparing notes find that they heard remarkably similar things, they are entitled to the view that the reason is the common-sense one that they all heard the same person speaking over the airwaves.

The fifth and last is 'the postulate of analogy', which states that 'given two classes of events A and B, and given that, whenever both A and B can be observed, there is reason to believe that A causes B, then if, in a given case, A is observed, but there is no way of observing whether B occurs or not, it is probable that B occurs; and similarly if B is observed, but the presence or absence of A cannot be observed'. This postulate speaks for itself (*HK* 506–12).

The point of the postulates is, Russell says, to justify the first steps towards science. They state what we have to know, in addition to observed facts, if scientific inferences are to be valid. It is not advanced science which is thus justified, but its more elementary parts, themselves based on common-sense experience.

But what is the sense of 'know' here? On Russell's view, the knowing involved in 'knowledge of the postulates' is a kind of 'animal knowing', which arises as habitual beliefs from the experience of interaction with the world. It is far from being certain knowledge. 'Owing to the world being such as it is,' Russell says:

certain occurrences are sometimes, in fact, evidence for certain others; and owing to animals being adapted to their environment, occurrences which are, in fact, evidence of others tend to arouse expectation of those others. By reflecting on this process and refining it, we arrive at the canons of inductive inference. These canons are valid if the world has certain characteristics which we all believe it to have. (*HK* 514–15)

These characteristics are the common-sense facts that the postulates in effect embody, and it is in this sense that we 'know' them. They are implied in the inferences we make, and our inferences are by and large successful; so the postulates can be regarded as in a sense self-confirming.

Although Russell thinks of the postulates as something we know a priori, it is clear that their status is odd. They are in fact empirical in one sense, since they either record or are suggested by experience. What gives them their a priori status is that they are *treated as known* independently of empirical confirmation (except indirectly in practice), rather than as generalizations in need of such justification. In effect Russell has selected some general contingent beliefs which are especially useful to have as premisses in thinking about the world, and elevated them to the dignity of postulates. Their indirect justification, in turn, is that on the whole they, or the results of their application, work. Allied to the extremely modest ambition Russell has for epistemology in *HK*—it is no longer the quest for as certain a basis for knowledge as one can get, but only a statement of rules of thumb whose adoption makes scientific thinking acceptable—this might be enough. But it has no pretensions to be a response to scepticism, or a rigorous account of non-demonstrative reasoning.

These last remarks suggest why Russell's arguments in *HK* received little response, much to his disappointment. He recognized well enough that canons of evidence and scientific reasoning are worth investigating only if we can be confident that, if we get them right, they will deliver substantial contingent knowledge about the world. But the most that Russell's argument establishes is that, so far, the general principles on which our empirical thinking relies have been largely successful. But this looks like exactly the kind of unbuttressed inductive inference Russell was anxious to caution against, citing the example of the chicken who, on being fed day after day, grew increasingly pleased with the world—until the day of her encounter with the butcher. There are limits to pragmatic justification; imagine someone who encourages the growth of his tomatoes by prayer alone, and gets some tomatoes every year, and someone else who waters and fertilizes his tomatoes, and gets many more each year; still, the first gardener might regard the fact that he gets some tomatoes as pragmatic justification for praying over them. The success of our principles to date does not, thus, amount to much of a ground for saying that they deliver the scientific goods.

In particular, we have no guarantee against the possibility that use of the postulates leads us to falsehood, either occasionally or in some systematic way concealed by the kind of situation exemplified by the praying gardener. Now this possibility is in effect allowed by Russell in asking very little of epistemology. The complaint must therefore be that the argument in *HK* is in fact an admission of failure, when taken in the light of the epistemological tradition. Descartes and his successors in modern philosophy raised questions about the nature of knowledge and how we get it precisely so that they could distinguish between some enterprises—alchemy, astrology, and magic, say—and others —chemistry, astronomy, and medicine, say—which differ not merely in the number of really useful applications they offer, but in telling us something true about the world; and where, moreover, the latter fact explains the former, and opens the way to more of both by the same route. Furthermore, our ancient prejudices and animal beliefs might be controverted in the process, as indeed happens: for the world depicted by science is remarkably different from the world of common sense. But Russell in *HK* says that the utility of applications and those same animal habits of belief are the only final justifiers we can hope for in epistemology. This is very much less than the project of epistemology traditionally aims to achieve, and it is much less than Russell himself hoped to attain when he first took up the epistemological task many decades before.

4 Politics and Society

Introduction

Russell contributed voluminously to debates about morals, politics, religion, education, and questions of war and peace. He did not think of these contributions as being in the strict sense philosophical. As the preceding chapter shows, he regarded philosophy as a technical discipline concerned with abstract questions about logic, knowledge, and metaphysics. These other debates, in his opinion, are by contrast matters of emotion and opinion, relating as they do to practicalities of life. He acknowledged that there can be analysis of moral and political discourse in a formal sense, that is, as a systematic study dealing with their logic rather than their substance; but it was practical questions and concrete problems that interested him, especially after the outbreak of the First World War.

Nevertheless, in certain of his writings Russell ventured an account of the basis of ethics. He did not try to state an original theory, resting content with consciously derivative views which (after his interest in practical questions had become serious) were 'consequentialist' in character, having it that the moral worth of what people and governments do must be judged by outcomes. At the same time—and not altogether consistently—he sometimes wrote as if he believed in the intrinsic moral worth of certain things, such as the character traits of courage, magnanimity, and honesty. And he also, in some of his earlier writings, put forward a view further inconsistent with these, that moral judgements are disguised statements of subjective attitude. The main problem for Russell was how to reconcile two conflicting things: on the one hand, allegiance to profoundly and passionately held moral convictions, and, on the other hand, the apparent groundlessness of moral judgement. His difficulty in achieving this reconciliation was increased by his scepticism about whether there can be such a thing as ethical knowledge at all.

The best way to characterize Russell's contribution in the ethical sphere is, perhaps, to say that he was much more a moralist than a moral philosopher. Like Aristotle before him he regarded ethics and politics as continuous; there is no difference of kind between the ethical judgement that war is evil and the political demand for peace. Accordingly there is a seamlessness in Russell's thinking about morality, politics, and society which explains why, in the most thorough of his books on these questions, *Human Society in Ethics and Politics (HSEP)*, they are considered together.

In politics Russell was all his life a radical and, in the small 'l' sense, a liberal. After the First World War he became a member of the Labour Party and stood as its candidate in two elections. He tore up his membership card in the 1960s in disgust at Harold Wilson's support for American war-making in Vietnam. But he was never a socialist in the old-fashioned sense, having been unpersuaded by Marxism when he studied it in Germany in the 1890s for his first book, *German Social Democracy* ('social democracy' then denoted Marxism). He was temperamentally opposed to the centralizing tendency of socialism as then understood— which was practically the only aspect of socialism (or 'socialism') ever put fully into practice in the Soviet world—and was accordingly much more attracted by Guild Socialism, a highly decentralized form of co-operative ownership and control in which people govern themselves in circumstances that, in the ideal, integrate their social, recreational, and working lives.

Russell was at his best when criticizing contemporary moral and political conditions. The positive alternatives he suggested typically look unpersuasive, tending to be either utopian or, at very least—given the circumstances in which he offered them— impracticable to a degree. But as critic, scourge, and gadfly he is in the league of Socrates and Voltaire.

No one needs an excuse or a license to contribute to debate on the great questions of society—the questions of politics, morals, and education. It is, arguably, a civic duty to be an informed participant. Russell's activities in these respects therefore need no justification. But there is a good reason why his contributions have a certain authority. It is that he was better equipped than many for the task This is not because he was an inheritor of a grand Whig tradition of involvement in public affairs, although no doubt this prompted both his interest in them and his sense of obligation to take part. Rather it was because his interest and sense of obligation were supported by four priceless assets: an extraordinary intelligence, a lucid eloquence, a broad knowledge of history, and complete fearlessness in the face of opposition. This made him a formidable debater. It was only at the end of his life, when others around him were speaking and writing in his name, that he sounded shrill and ill-judging.

Some of his ideas, such as belief in world government, have so far found little support. Others helped transform the social landscape of the Western world, as, for example, in attitudes to marriage and sexual morality. In other spheres again—not least in connection with religion—Russell liberated many minds, but he would not be surprised, given his understanding of human nature, to find that superstition flourishes even more now than in his day, and that dogma—'faith is what I die for, dogma is what I kill for'—is back with a vengeance.

Theoretical Ethics

In his very earliest thinking about ethics Russell held the romantic Hegelian view that the universe is good in itself and a fit object for 'intellectual love'. His acceptance of this view was inspired by McTaggart, but it did not retain its hold on him for long. His first serious treatment of ethical questions, set out in his paper 'The Elements of Ethics' and published in 1910, shows Russell following the teaching of G. E. Moore's *Principia Ethica*, in which Moore argues that goodness is an indefinable, unanalysable, but objective property of things, actions, and people, which we perceive by an act of direct moral intuition. Moore held a version of utilitarianism, which can be summarized as the view that the right thing to do in any given case is whatever will result in promoting the greatest balance of good over ill in that case. Moore's views were influential among members of the Bloomsbury set, not least in promoting the attractive idea that friendship and the enjoyment of beauty are the highest ethical goods. (Unkind critics claimed that the Bloomsburies liked this view because they could economize—so to speak—by having beautiful friends.)

Difficulties immediately suggest themselves in connection with the utilitarian view. One is that we cannot know fully what the consequences will be of acting one way rather than another, and therefore we might inadvertently promote bad consequences as a result of muddled thinking or mistaken intuitions. In his version of Moore's view Russell acknowledges this, but argues that we have acted rightly when we are satisfied that we have thought matters through carefully, and done our best on the available information. The claim that goodness is objective, however, is another matter, and Russell could not be content with it for long, for although it might, strictly speaking, be irrefutable, neither can it be proved correct, most significantly in the face of someone who flatly disagrees with another's intuition that goodness is present in such-and-such an act or situation.

This difficulty led Russell to adopt the view, expressed in *An Outline of Philosophy* (1927), that moral judgements are not objective—that is, are not true or false—but are instead disguised imperatives, optatives, or statements of attitude. An imperative is a command, such as 'do not tell lies'; an optative is a choice or wish—as when one opts for one thing rather than another—in the ethical case expressible by 'would that no one told untruths'; and 'I disapprove of lying' is a report of its utterer's attitude to lying. Imperatives and optatives obviously lack truth-value. Although matters are otherwise with reports of attitudes, this is only because they are descriptions of the relevant psychological fact about their possessors; nothing true or false is being said about the moral value of lying, only about what the speaker thinks of lying.

This position might, to contrast it with Moore's objectivism, be called 'subjectivism'. It suffers from equally grave problems, not the least of which is that it is straightforwardly implausible. Consider, say, the Holocaust. It is intolerable to think that one's ground for judging that the Holocaust is evil is merely that one disapproves of it. Russell felt this difficulty acutely, and therefore in his final and fullest discussion of these questions (*HSEP*) tried to find a half-way position between objectivism and subjectivism which has the benefits but avoids the difficulties of both.

Moral judgements, he argues in *HSEP*, are in reality judgements about the good of society and its individual members. Such judgements embody or express the fairly widespread community of feeling in a given society about what, generally speaking, is in everyone's interests. And this is a matter about which there can be sensible debate based on a scientific or at least rational understanding of the world. This belief in the possibility of rational resolutions to moral dilemmas often threatened to desert Russell when he contemplated human folly, but he clung to it nevertheless.

The fundamental data of ethics, Russell says, are feelings and emotions. Accordingly, ethical judgements are disguised expressions of our hopes, fears, desires, or aversions. We judge things to be good when they satisfy our desires. Therefore the general good— the good of society as a whole—consists in the total satisfaction of desire, no matter by whom enjoyed. By the same token the good of any section of society consists in the overall satisfaction of its members' desires; and an individual's good consists in the satisfaction of his personal desires. On this basis one can define 'right action' by saying that it is whatever, on any given occasion, is most likely to promote the general good (or if it concerns only an individual, that individual's good); and this in turn gives us our explanation of moral obligation, the idea that there are things that one 'ought' to do; which is, simply, that one ought to do the right thing as thus understood (*HSEP* 25, 51, 60, 72).

Russell of course recognizes that there are difficulties with this account, and discusses a number of them. For example: the definition of 'good' as 'satisfaction of desire' invites the obvious objection that some desires are evil, and that satisfying them is a worse evil. Russell considers the example of cruelty. Can it be good if someone wishes to make another suffer? And is it not even worse if he succeeds in carrying out his wish? Russell says that his definition does not imply that such a state of affairs is good. For one thing, it involves the frustration of the victim's desires, for the victim naturally desires to avoid suffering at the perpetrator's hands. And for another, society at large will not in general desire that its members should be victims of cruelty, and so its desires in this respect will be frustrated too. Accordingly there will be a great preponderance of unfulfilled desire when cruelty is perpetrated, thus making it bad.

Another difficulty for Russell's account is that desires can conflict. He responds by saying that this places a demand on us to choose desires that will be least likely to compete with one another. Borrowing a technical term from Leibniz, Russell calls consistency between desires their 'compossibility'. Good and bad desires can then be defined as those which are compossible with, respectively, as many and as few other desires as possible.

Russell devotes a chapter to the question whether judgements such as 'cruelty is wrong' are simply disguised expressions of subjective attitude. As noted, this question is important, and it troubled Russell deeply. He arrived at what might be called his 'sociological' answer—that moral value is the product of a kind of social consensus—after considering alternative possibilities offered by ethical debate.

The problem can be stated by noting that the chief difference between ordinary factual discourse and moral discourse is the presence in the latter of terms like 'ought', 'good', and their synonyms. Are these terms part of the 'minimum vocabulary' of ethics, that is, both indefinable and fundamental to any understanding of ethical concepts; or can they be defined in terms of something else, for example feelings and emotions? And if this latter, are the sentiments in question those of the individual who makes a moral judgement, or do they have a reference more generally to the desires and feelings of mankind? (*HSEP* 110–11).

In discussing these questions Russell notes that when we examine moral disagreements over what ought to be done in a given case, we find that many of them derive from disagreement over what will result from this or that course of action. This shows that moral evaluations turn on estimates of outcomes, and that therefore we can define 'ought' by saying that an act ought to be performed if, among all acts possible in the case, it is the one most likely to produce the greatest amount of 'intrinsic value' (an expression Russell uses as a more precise substitute for 'good').

Is 'intrinsic value' definable? Russell thinks it is. 'When we examine the things to which we are inclined to attach intrinsic value,' he says, 'we find that they are all things that are desired or enjoyed. It is difficult to believe that anything would have intrinsic value in a universe devoid of sentience. This suggests that "intrinsic value" may be definable in terms of desire or pleasure or both' (*HSEP* 113). Since not all desires can be intrinsically valuable because desires conflict, Russell refines the notion so that intrinsic value is understood as a property of the 'states of mind' desired by those who experience them.

With this adjustment, Russell offers the following summary of his view. As a rule our approval or otherwise of given acts is dependent on what consequences we think they are likely to have. The consequences of acts we approve we call 'good', their opposites 'bad'. The acts themselves we call 'right' and 'wrong' respectively. What we 'ought' to do is whatever is a right act in the circumstances, that is, whatever will produce the greatest balance of good.

Of these points the first carries greatest weight. If moral evaluation is a matter of what people approve and disapprove, are we not marooned in the subjectivist dilemma, without rational grounds for committing ourselves to the wrongness of, say, racism, intolerance, cruelty, and the rest? Russell's answer is that there is as a matter of fact widespread agreement among people about what is desirable. He agrees with Henry Sidgwick that the acts which people generally approve are those which produce most happiness or pleasure. If this includes the satisfaction of intellectual and aesthetic interests ('If we were really persuaded that pigs are happier than human beings, we should not on that account welcome the ministrations of Circe'; some pleasures are *inherently* preferable to others), then we have our escape from subjectivism; for this view gives us statements about what ought to be done which are not merely disguised optatives or imperatives, and thus have truth-value; but which, nevertheless, rest on facts about our feelings and the satisfaction of our desires. Facts about our feelings underlie the definition of 'right' and 'wrong', and facts about satisfaction of desires underlie the definition of 'intrinsic value'. Thus Russell claims success in having articulated a half-way position between objectivism and subjectivism which, at the same time, has practical credentials in a quite straightforward sense, as providing a way of evaluating not just actions of the kind typically at issue in moral debates, but social customs, laws, and government policies.

Despite Russell's optimism about this view, it contains a number of difficulties. In effect it says that the basis of evaluation is consensus of desire. But this means that if the majority in a given society is offended by, say, homosexuality, homosexuality will accordingly count as bad, whereas in a more tolerant society where a different consensus holds, homosexuality will not be bad. Is moral relativism of this degree plausible? This difficulty is related to another, which is that because the value of consequences is measured by how much they satisfy desires, the degree of the Holocaust's evil is a function of the degree to which the satisfaction of Nazi desires is outweighed by the frustration of their victim's desires and those of the generality of the world's population, who might not wish genocide to become commonplace (perhaps in case they become victims of it). Russell himself felt that something more compelling underlies the moral horror we feel in the face of the Holocaust, but his principles do not explain it.

Any familiarity with debate in ethics shows that Russell's efforts in the field are sketchy. Even in *HSEP* the discussion is less philosophical than exhortatory. Based on broad psychological generalities, with only a gesture towards rigour, the aim of *HSEP* is to get us to accept a practical method of ethical evaluation rather than to provide ethics with a theoretical foundation. Part of the reason, as noted, is that Russell did not believe rigour can be applied to discussion of ethics; originally the ethical chapters in *HSEP* were to have been a continuation of *Human Knowledge*, but he held them back, dissatisfied, and only published them, supplemented by chapters on political questions, after at last deciding that he could not make the arguments they contain more systematic. But he did not repine; his chief aim in ethics, as with all the social questions he addressed, was after all a polemical one. He wished to influence how people live, and to that end was content to commit himself in the main to advocacy and persuasion.

Practical Morality

Russell's Nobel Prize was awarded to him for literature, and the book cited was *Marriage and Morals*. Russell wrote much on practical moral questions, some of the best of it to be found in the dozens of short pieces he contributed to newspapers, not least those published by the Hearst Press in America during the early 1930s. In these pieces (invariably seven hundred and fifty words long, as required by the size of the column reserved for them on the newspaper page) Russell comes across as remarkably observant, tolerant, humane, and sensible—and on many questions a long way ahead not only of his time but ours.

Take, for example, his essay 'On Tact'. We put tact and truth-fulness in quite separate boxes, he observes, but this carries a certain cost.

I have sometimes passed children playing in the park and heard them say in a loud clear voice, 'Mummy, who is that funny old man?' To which comes a shocked, subdued, 'Hush! Hush!' The children become dimly aware that they have done something wrong, but are completely at a loss to imagine what it is. All children occasionally get presents that they do not like and are instructed by their parents that they must seem delighted with them. As they are also informed that they ought not to tell lies, the result is moral confusion. ('On Tact', in *Mortals and Others* (London: Allen & Unwin, 1975), i. 158)

Such is an education in tact. Tact is undoubtedly a virtue, Russell says, but only the thinnest of lines separates it from hypocrisy. The distinction is one of motive. If kindliness prompts us to please another in circumstances where bluntness might cause upset, tact is appropriate; but it is less amiable when the motive is fear of offending, or desire to obtain an advantage by flattery. People who are profoundly earnest dislike tact; when Beethoven visited Goethe in Weimar he was shocked to see him behaving politely to a set of foolish courtiers. People who are always sincere, and never tell polite lies, are generally appreciated, but this, says Russell, is because genuinely sincere people are free from envy, malice, and pettiness. 'Most of us have a dose of these vices in our composition, and therefore have to exercise tact to avoid giving offence. We cannot all be saints, and if saintliness is impossible, we may at least try not to be too disagreeable.'

This may be slight stuff, but it is perceptive, and makes points worth considering. Russell's journalism on social questions is characteristically like this: enjoyable, amusing, and instructive.

Marriage and Morals deals with larger and more pressing questions. It focuses upon sex and family life. In Russell's view, sexual morality has two principal sources: men's desire to be sure that they are truly the fathers of the children to whom their women give birth, and the religion-inspired belief that sex is sinful. Russell was always prepared to take instruction from the science of his day, in this instance looking to biology for an explanation of the origins of custom. It prompted him to think that sexual morality in early times had the biological purpose of securing the protection of two parents for each child, a motive which Russell is keen to agree is a good one. Many pressures threaten modern family life, he says, and ought to be resisted. Children need the affection of both their parents; the alternative, which is to leave the upbringing of children partly or even wholly to the state, as Plato wished, has little to recommend it. If the state were to bring up children the result would be too much uniformity, and perhaps too much harshness; and children thus raised would be fertile recruits for political propagandists and demagogues.

But so far as personal sexual morality is concerned, in Russell's view, the modern tendency to greater freedom of opinion and action is a good thing. Freer opinions result from a loosening of the grip of traditional morality, especially religious morality; and freer action is made possible by improvements in contraception, which put women on a par with men in having control over their sexual lives.

In Russell's opinion the doctrine that sex is sinful has done untold harm. The harm begins in childhood and continues into adulthood in the form of inhibitions and the stresses they cause. By repressing sexual impulses, conventional morality subverts other kinds of friendly feeling also, making people less generous and kindly, and more prone to self-assertion and cruelty. Sex of course must be governed by an ethic, just as business or sport has to be, but it should not be based on 'ancient prohibitions propounded by uneducated people in a society totally unlike our own'—by which Russell means the teachings of the Church fathers long ago. 'In sex, as in economics and in politics, our ethic is still dominated by fears which modern discoveries have made irrational' (*MM* 196–7).

A new morality, premissed on rejection of traditional Puritanism, must be based on the belief that instinct should be trained, not thwarted. A freer attitude to sexual life does not imply that we can simply follow our impulses and do as we like. This is because there has to be consistency in life, and some of our most worthwhile efforts are those directed at long-term goals, which means the deferral of short-term gratifications. Moreover, there has to be consideration for others and 'standards of rectitude'. But, Russell argues, self-control is not an end in itself, and moral conventions should make the need for it a minimum rather than a maximum. It can be the former if the instincts are well directed from childhood onwards. Traditional moralists think that because the sexual instincts are powerful they have to be severely checked in childhood, for fear that they will become anarchic and gross. But a good life cannot be based on anxieties and prohibitions.

The general principles on which Russell thinks sexual morality ought to be founded are therefore simple and few. First, sexual relationships should be based on 'as much as possible of that deep, serious love between man and woman which embraces the whole personality of both and leads to a fusion by which each is en-riched and enhanced'. And secondly, if children result, they should be adequately cared for physically and psychologically. Neither of these principles is particularly shocking, Russell remarks with a certain wryness, conscious of the opprobrium he had earned for adultery, divorce, unmarried cohabitation, and insouciance about keeping them out of public view, all mightily scandalous at the time. But together the principles imply certain important adjust-ments to the conventional moral code.

One is that it permits a measure of what is usually called 'infi-delity'. If people were not brought up to think of sex as hedged about by taboos, and if jealousy did not have the sanction of mor-alists, then people would be capable of more wholehearted and generous attitudes towards each other. Jealousy makes couples keep one another in a mutual prison, as if it gave each a right over the other's person and needs. 'Unfaithfulness should not be treated as something terrible', wrote Russell, for the existence of 'confid-ence in the ultimate strength of a deep and permanent affection' is a far better tie than jealousy (*MM* 200–1). Elsewhere Russell argues that there can be no objection to open marriage, as such an arrangement is sometimes called, provided that the woman does not have children by a lover which her husband is expected to raise. His own marriage to Dora ended partly because of this problem.

Russell concludes *MM* by saying that the doctrine he is offering is not, despite these remarks on fidelity, one of licence; indeed, it involves nearly as much self-control as conventional morality demands, with the large difference that the self-control is to be exercised in abstaining from interference with the freedom of others rather than in restraining one's own freedom. 'It may, I think, be hoped', Russell wrote, 'that with the right education from the start this respect for the personality and freedom of others may become comparatively easy; but for those of us who have been brought up to think that we have a right to place a veto upon the actions of others in the name of virtue, it is undoubtedly difficult to forgo the exercise of this agreeable form of persecution.' The essence of a good marriage is mutual respect and deep intimacy. Where these exist, serious love between man and woman is 'the most fructifying of all human experiences'; and that is what all thinking about marriage and morals should aim to promote (*MM* 202–3).

Many at the time found Russell's views profoundly shocking. *Marriage and Morals* lost him his job in New York in 1940 (although ten years later, as noted, it earned him a Nobel Prize, which illustrates how unpredictable life can be), and together with his reputation for enjoying female company it led many to attach to him the character of a satyr. But two points might be noted about these views. One is their calm and tolerant good sense. The other is that they did not spring out of the blue; they are in fact expressive of an attitude shared by the vanguard of left-wing intellectuals in the 1920s and 1930s, for whom free love and rejection of sexual jealousy were unwritten principles. Russell had the courage and crisp logical eloquence required to put these ideas forward in the hope of letting fresh air into an area of life badly needing it. Despite the revolution in attitudes and practices which occurred a generation later, in part made possible by Russell's advocacy, his arguments are still worth reading as a specific against reaction.

In Russell's views on human relationships three topics frequently recur. One is the harmfulness of religion, another is the need for good education, and the third is individual liberty. Each is a constant theme in Russell's social thought, and to each he devoted considerable attention. I consider them in turn.

Religion

It comes as a surprise to people when they learn that Russell was not an atheist. He was, instead, an agnostic. Consistency demanded of him that he accept the *possibility* that there might be deity, but he thought that the existence of such a thing is highly improbable, and moreover, that if there were such a thing—especially if it were anything like the God of Christian orthodoxy—the moral repugnance of the universe would be even greater than it is, because then we would have to accept either that an omnipotent being allows, or that it wills, the existence of natural and moral evil in the world ('natural evil' denotes disease, catastrophes such as earthquakes and hurricanes, and the like). On Russell's view, a visit to the wards of any children's hospital should be enough to make one feel either that there cannot be a deity, or that if there is one, it is a monster.

Russell was famously asked what he would do if, upon dying, he discovered that God exists after all. He replied that he would take God to task for not providing sufficient evidence of his existence. He was also asked what he thought of 'Pascal's wager'. This is the view that we should believe in God even though the evidence for his existence is extremely small, because the advantage of doing so, if God exists, far outweighs the disadvantage if he does not. Russell replied that if God exists he would approve of unbelievers who used their brains and saw that the evidence in favour of belief is inadequate.

A standard technique for Russell was to refuse to accept a proposition unless there is good reason for doing so. A central part of the case in natural theology for the proposition that God exists ('natural theology' means discussion of the concept of deity independently of particular revelations in scripture or mystical experience) is the set of well-known 'proofs of God's existence'. Russell discusses them in *Why I Am Not A Christian* (1957, first delivered as lectures in 1927).

One is the First Cause argument, which says that everything has a cause, so there must be a first cause. But this, says Russell, is inconsistent, because if everything has a cause how can the first cause be uncaused? On some views, God is the self-caused cause (in Aristotle, the self-moved mover), but either this notion is incoherent, or if it denotes something possible, then either the principle of universal causation upon which the whole argument rests is false if causes must be other than their effects (as indeed the principle seems to imply), or, if causes can be their own causes, why should there be only one such?

A second argument draws from the appearance of design in the universe the conclusion that there must be a Designer. But for one thing the appearance of design in things is better explained by evolution, which involves no extra entities in the universe, and fits the empirical data; and for another there is anyway no evidence of *overall* design in the world, where the facts—consistently with the second law of thermodynamics, which tells us that the world is in effect decaying—suggest quite the contrary.

A third argument is that there has to be a deity to provide grounds for morality. This will not do, however, because, as Russell elsewhere succinctly argues, 'Theologians have always taught that God's decrees are good, and that this is not a mere tautology: it follows that goodness is logically independent of God's decrees' (*HSEP* 48). It might be added that if the will of a deity is taken to be the ground of morality, then one's reason for being moral is a prudential one merely; it consists in a desire to escape punishment. But this is hardly a satisfactory basis for the moral life, and anyway threats are not *logically* compelling premises for any argument.

A related argument, employed by Kant, is that there must be a God to reward virtue and punish evil, because it is clear from experience that in this life virtue is not always or even often guaranteed a reward. But this, says Russell, is like saying that because all the oranges at the top of the crate are rotten, the oranges further down must be good; which is absurd.

Many opponents of religion, while decrying its evil effect in the world as a promoter of persecution and discord, nevertheless find Jesus Christ an attractive figure. Russell did not. He thought him less gentle and compassionate than Buddha and far inferior to Socrates in intellect and character. Some of his behaviour is uncongenial, as when he blasted the fig tree—which could hardly have helped being fruitless, since it was out of season—and threatened to visit eternal agonies on those who would not believe in him. Russell pointed out that for many centuries, just so long as it served the interests of the Church, people were encouraged to believe in the literal truth of these bloodthirsty warnings. But when in a more humane age critics pointed out how repulsive they are, the Church shifted to saying that they are to be understood only metaphorically.

But it is against Christianity as an *organized* phenomenon that Russell most directed his fire. He hated superstition—'The Roman Catholic Church holds that a priest can turn a piece of bread into the body and blood of Christ by talking Latin to it'— and its sheer illogicality—'We are told not to work on Saturdays, and Protestants take this to mean that we are not to play on Sundays'. In Russell's view, Christianity is distinguished above other religions in its readiness for persecution. Christians have harrassed and killed heretics, Jews, freethinkers, and one another; they have drowned, burned, and otherwise murdered thousands of innocent women accused of 'witchcraft'; and they have blighted the lives of hundreds of millions with their preposterous doctrines about sin and sexuality.

Russell's weapons in the war on religion were chiefly mockery and disdain. He knew the Bible better than many of his opponents, and could confound them with apt quotation; as when he remarks, in discussing the relative merits of religion and science, that 'the Bible tells us that the hare chews the cud', which causes difficulties for fundamentalists faced with zoology. Indeed the contrast between religion and science could not be more marked. Religion deals in absolute and incontrovertible truths which hold good for eternity; science is more cautious and tentative. Religion imposes limits on thought, forbidding enquiry when it conflicts with what the Church lays down; science is open-minded (*Religion and Science*, 14–16). These are telling contrasts. In the face of scientific reason the best that religion can do, when it does not try to remain obdurately fundamentalist, is to reinterpret its scriptures in allegorical vein, and to hide behind the claim that religious truths surpass human understanding.

But although Russell was hostile to religion, he was nevertheless a religious man. This is only a seeming paradox. It is possible to have a religious attitude to life without belief in supernatural beings and occurrences. Such an attitude is one in which appreciation of art, love, and knowledge brings nourishment to the human spirit, and carries with it a sense of awe before the world and those one loves, and a concomitant sense of the immensity of which one is part. In a famous if stylistically overblown essay, 'A Free Man's Worship', written under the influence of the failure of his first marriage and concomitant changes in outlook, Russell sets out just such a vision. But it carries dark qualifications:

> When first the opposition of fact and ideal grows fully visible, a spirit of fiery revolt, of fierce hatred of the gods, seems necessary to the assertion of freedom. To defy with Promethean constancy a hostile universe, to keep its evil always in view, always actively hated, to refuse no pain the malice of Power can invent, appears to be the duty of all who will not bow before the inevitable. But indignation is still a bondage, for it compels our thoughts to be occupied with an evil world; and in the fierceness of desire from which rebellion springs there is a kind of self-assertion which it is necessary for the wise to overcome. Indignation is a submission of our thoughts, but not of our desires; the Stoic freedom in which wisdom consists is found in the submission of our desires, but not of our thoughts. From the submission of our desires springs the virtue of resignation; from the freedom of our thoughts springs the whole world of art and philosophy, and the vision of beauty by which, at last, we half reconquer the reluctant world. ('A Free Man's Worship', 1903, reprinted in *Mysticism and Logic*)

As this shows, the yearning for transcendence—for Spinoza's dream of an utterly clear, dispassionate, synoptic understanding of all things that will set one free—was always tempered for Russell by the hard facts of suffering in the world. In the 'Prologue' to his autobiography he writes: 'Love and knowledge, so far as they were possible, led upward to the heavens. But always pity brought me back to earth.' In his agnostic way, therefore, Russell yearned for the heavens, and strove to find pathways that would lead mankind there.

Education

The chief of those pathways, Russell hoped, was education, which for him was a question of how people should be equipped for life. He did not address himself to administrative details about the provision of schools and universities and the training of teachers, as Sydney and Beatrice Webb might have done, but talked instead of what might be called the spiritual (again: in a secular sense) goals of education. The aim of education, he wrote, is to form character; and the best kind of character is vital, courageous, sensitive, and intelligent, all 'to the highest degree'. This is how he puts matters in *On Education*, published in 1926, a year before he and Dora founded Beacon Hill School. This book deals mainly with the earliest childhood years, and in his autobiography Russell acknowledges that he was 'unduly optimistic in his psychology' and in some ways also 'unduly harsh' in the methods he proposed. An example might be the view, adopted from Montessori principles, that if a child behaves badly it should be isolated from other children until it learns to be good. Russell later came to think this a cruel form of discipline.

The book nevertheless contains some sound advice. Starting with the very young, Russell argues that babies should have a regular routine and be provided with as many opportunities for learning as possible, but that any parental anxieties should be carefully concealed lest they 'pass to the child by suggestion'. This tenet reflects Russell's belief that since anxiety is not instinctive among other higher mammals, its appearance in children must be the result of their learning it from adults. At the same time he reminded readers not to martyr themselves to parenthood, but to strike an appropriate balance between their own interests and those of their children.

Russell believed that knowledge is in itself both liberating and a safeguard against fear. A lively interest in outward things—a central theme also of his *Conquest of Happiness*—is a powerful help to courageous and joyous living. Russell also advises on how to promote truthfulness and generosity: not by relying on punishment of their opposites—since what might on the face of things seem to be, say, lying might in fact be the exercise of imagination—but by encouraging the positive traits when they appear. It was in this regard, as he later recognized, that he might have been too optimistic about the psychology of the young. His experience as a schoolmaster soon taught him that children are capable of wickedness, and that if wickedness is left unpunished it can, as in *Lord of the Flies*, grow monstrous.

But even in these early views Russell was not wedded to *laissez-faire* principles, especially not in connection with study. He believed that the acquisition of habits of self-discipline and concentration would prove liberating in the long run, and although he argued that the attention of children should be engaged by attracting rather than coercing them to their schoolwork, he was not against applying their noses to the grindstone when necessary. Children should be able to read by 5, he said, and should make an early start on a couple of languages. The rudiments of mathematics need drilling, and it should be given. Poetry and plays can be enjoyed at primary school age, but real appreciation of literature only comes later. Classics, history, and science come later still; by this stage the pupil, after having tried these subjects, should choose whichever seems most interesting, and follow it up for himself or herself (*OE* 18–162).

These views on the curriculum are conventional enough. What was not conventional, and therefore caused scandal at the time, was what Russell had to say about sex education. Instant legends sprang up about Beacon Hill School; a representative tale has a bishop arriving at the door and exclaiming, on being met by a naked child, 'My God!', to which the naked child replies, 'There is no God'. But in fact all Russell argued was that children should not be made anxious about their bodies, and should therefore be calmly informed of the mechanics of sex before puberty arrives, a good reason for the early start being that they will not therefore learn about sex in inappropriate and fevered ways. In surprisingly conventional line with medical opinion of the day Russell was doubtful whether masturbation is a good thing, so on this matter at least he can hardly be accused of dangerous opinions.

Five years later, after first-hand experience in his own school, Russell wrote *Education and the Social Order* (1931). In it he held to most of what he had said in *On Education*, but now labelled it the 'negative' theory and admitted that it needed supplementation. The negative theory says that the task in education is to provide opportunities and remove barriers so that children can develop in their own ways. Russell now saw that what is further required is that children should receive positive instruction in getting along with others. He had been shocked by episodes of bullying at Beacon Hill, and saw it as a microcosm of the brutal behaviour of adults, and indeed of whole nations. His anxiety that irrationality and aggression are innate was deepened by the experience, and it made him despair for the world because it seemed to suggest that nationalism and war are inevitabilities of the human condition.

Russell never had inflated expectations of education. But despite the disillusionment prompted by his practical experiment in school-teaching, he retained his characteristic liberal belief that it is chiefly on education that hopes for a better world must focus. In his popular writings on social and political questions Russell was indeed tirelessly attempting to do just that: to educate, with the whole world as his classroom. Despite everything, he never lost hope that vital, brave, sensitive, and intelligent people could be brought into being if only they are given the right kind of guidance in childhood.

Politics

If we are to understand politics, Russell held, we must understand power. All political institutions are historically rooted in authority; at first, the authority of a tribal leader or king, to whom people submitted out of fear; later, to the institution of kingship, to which people gave allegiance as a matter of custom. Russell disagreed with those who held that civil society arose from an original 'social contract' in which individuals gave up part of their freedom in return for the benefits—not least among them security—of social living. If there were any original contract, he said, it was one between members of the ruling élite, a 'contract among conquerors', to which they subscribed in order to consolidate their position and privileges (*Power*, 190).

In Russell's view, history suggests that monarchy constitutes the earliest type of developed political arrangement. Authority filtered down through the social hierarchy, from the king—who, in many dispensations, claimed to receive it from God—to the nobility, the gentry, and so on down to the humblest man at the head of his own family in his cottage. The advantages of the system, when it commanded the loyalty of those involved, was social cohesion. Its disadvantage is that the absolute ruler has no incentive to rule benevolently; there are many examples of such arrangements becoming tyrannical and cruel (*Power*, 189).

The natural successor to monarchy is oligarchy, Russell says, and this admits of a variety of forms: aristocracy, plutocracy, priesthoods, or political parties. Rule by the rich, as exemplified in the free cities of the Middle Ages and by Venice until Napoleon captured it, seemed to Russell to have worked rather well, but he did not think modern industrialists were up to the same mark (*Power*, 193). As with monarchy when it commands loyalty, both Church and party political oligarchies can generate social cohesion through the sharing of beliefs or ideology, but the great danger they pose is their threat to liberty. Such oligarchies cannot tolerate those who disagree with their views, nor can they permit the existence of institutions which might challenge their monopoly of power (*Power*, 195–6).

Nevertheless, Russell noted, there is a benefit to be had from oligarchic forms of government, provided that liberty can be secured under them, which is that they allow for the existence of a leisured class. The reason is that leisure is a condition for the flourishing of mental life—for literature, learning, and art. In the past this involved the sacrifice of the many, who had to toil long hours so that the few could enjoy the requisite freedoms. But if good use is made of modern technology, Russell believed, 'we could, within twenty years, abolish all abject poverty, quite half the illness in the world, the whole economic slavery which binds down nine-tenths of our population: we could fill the world with beauty and joy, and secure the reign of universal peace' (*Political Ideals*, 27). Russell made these utopian remarks in 1917, by way of lighting a candle in the darkness of war, but they are not entirely devoid of point: given the success of science and its intelligent use for peaceful purposes, there is no reason why more leisure, and therefore more of the conditions for creative and flourishing life, should not be possible for more people. Such a possibility undermines the argument for social structures which support a leisured class, and makes instead a strong claim of justice in favour of democracy.

Still, the difference between democracy and oligarchy is only a matter of degree, Russell observes, because even under democracy only a few people can hold real power. This made Russell cynical even about the vaunted British parliamentary model, in which the average Member of Parliament is in reality little more than voting fodder for his or her party. But the picture is not wholly bleak as regards democracy, for although it cannot guarantee good government, it can nevertheless prevent certain evils, chiefly by ensuring that no bad government can stay in power permanently (*Power*, 286).

The best thing about democracy for Russell is its association with 'the doctrine of personal liberty', which he valued highly. The doctrine consists of two aspects. The first is that one's liberty is protected by requirements of due process at law, which shields one from arbitrary arrest and punishment. The second is that there are areas of individual action which are independent of control by the authorities, including freedom of speech and religious belief. These freedoms are not without limits; in wartime, for example, it might be necessary to curb free speech in the interests of national security. Russell recognized that there can indeed be much tension between the interests of society as a whole and those of an individual who desires maximum freedom. 'It is not difficult for a government to concede freedom of thought when it can rely upon loyalty in action,' he remarked, 'but when it cannot, the matter is more difficult' (*Power*, 155).

For Russell, questions of political organization are crucially questions of economic organization. The early, pre-First World War, Russell was a champion of free trade, and he remained a supporter of free enterprise for the good reason that he was opposed to the over-accumulation of economic power in any one set of hands, whether of capitalists or governments. He saw no reason why people should not be wealthy if they had earned it, but was hostile to the idea of inherited wealth. Although he allied himself for most of his adult life with socialism, it was in a particularly qualified way. The role of government in economic affairs, he said, is to guard against economic injustices. But this is not best done by vesting ownership or control of the means of production in government hands, as in the Communist experiment of the Soviet countries. Rather, Russell was attracted by what in France is called Syndicalism and in England, Guild Socialism, the theory that factories should be managed by their own workers, and that industries should be organized into Guilds. These would pay a tax to the state in return for their raw materials, and otherwise would be free to arrange wages and working conditions and to sell their products. Further, the Guilds would between them elect a Congress, consumers of their products would elect a Parliament, and the two together would be the national sovereign body, determining taxes and acting as the highest court in the land to decide the interests of workers and consumers alike (*Roads to Freedom*,

91–2). To ensure that the existence of Guilds does not compromise freedom, especially of expression, Russell proposed that a small minimum wage should be paid to everyone irrespective of whether or not he works, so that each could be quite independent if he chose. Anyone who wished to have more than this minimum would work, and the more they worked the richer they could be. He shrugged off the obvious objection that the scheme would be impossible if people chose not to work, thus producing no tax revenue but still requiring their minimum wage, by saying that most of them would be drawn to work by the inducement of prosperity; and anyway conditions of work and life generally would be pleasant under Guild Socialism, so they will not mind doing it (ibid. 119–20).

The principle at issue in Guild Socialism is devolution of that key political commodity, *power*. In Russell's view, concentration of power, especially in government hands, increases the likelihood of war. Its dissipation among many groups and individuals is therefore highly desirable. 'The positive purposes of the State, over and above the preservation of order, ought as far as possible to be carried out, not by the State itself, but by independent organisations which should be left completely free so long as they satisfied the State that they were not falling below a necessary minimum' (*Principles of Social Reconstruction*, 75). Russell formulated this view relatively early in his political thinking, and kept faith with it thereafter. In *Power* he argued that there is more need than ever for safeguards against official tyranny, propaganda, and the police—in connection with whom he made the original suggestion that there should be, in effect, custodians of the custodians: one police force should carry out the normal business of gathering evidence necessary for arresting supposed criminals and putting them on trial, while the other should be devoted to gathering evidence to prove those same people innocent.

Allied to the decentralizing thrust of Russell's politics was his hostility to nationalism. Before the Second World War he attacked it as 'a stupid idea' and 'the most dangerous vice of our time', which threatened the destruction of Europe. After the Second World War he saw it repeating itself in the Soviet Union and America, only this time—because both possessed weapons of mass destruction—it was vastly more dangerous. The only sure antidote to nationalism and the threat it poses, he argued, is World Government.

On the face of it this belief hardly seems consistent with Russell's decentralizing beliefs, and he recognized the risk of placing military might in the hands of a single universal power. But he thought it infinitely preferable to more world wars, in which weapons of ever greater destructive capability would be used, with the likelihood of destroying life on earth. This seemed to Russell so great an evil that practically anything would be preferable. But a world government need not be merely a lesser of evils. A good way of maintaining a measure of control over it would be to devolve as much power, in all but military respects, to the smallest local units feasible. Nevertheless, said Russell, in the end:

[a] world-State or federation of States, if it is to be successful, will have to decide questions, not by the legal maxims which would be applied by the Hague tribunal, but as far as possible in the same sense in which they would be decided by war. The function of authority should be to render the appeal to force unnecessary, not to give decisions contrary to those which would be reached by force. (*Principles of Social Reconstruction*, 66)

How might a world government be brought into being? National governments are unlikely to wish to surrender their sovereignty for so utopian a vision. On Russell's view, the most likely method is that one power or power bloc will eventually gain control of the world, and de facto will constitute the world government. In Cold War terms, Nato and the Warsaw Pact—or more accurately, their respective principals—could be seen as vying to achieve this outcome. Russell likened it to the development of orderly government in medieval times: a king seizes power, and then, by a process of evolution, sovereignty is brought under more and more democratic control. He thought that such a process might happen in the case of world government. The 'substitution of order for anarchy in international relations, if it comes about, will come about through the superior power of some one nation or group of nations. And only after such a single Government has been constituted will it be possible for the evolution towards a democratic form of international Government to begin'. He thought this might take a hundred years, during which the international government would have begun to earn 'the degree of respect that will make it possible to base its power upon law and sentiment rather than upon force' (*New Hopes For A Changing World*, 77–8).

A theme in all Russell's thinking about politics and government is the problem of balancing individual freedom and the need for international peace. But in the end the contest between them is an unequal one. There is not only no such freedom, but not even the possibility of such freedom, if mankind is destroyed by war. Accordingly Russell was prepared to see freedom compromised or delayed in the interests of saving humanity. Naturally he wished that peace and freedom could be secured together; but his experience of men had obliged him to accept that greed, brutality, irrationality, and other common human characteristics make this unlikely. This thought, he wrote, often drowned him in despair. It had done so during the First World War, as hundreds of thousands of men were driven to useless mutual slaughter in the mud of Europe. How much more did it do so after the Second World War, when the potential victims of nuclear weapons are no longer just armies, or even nations, but—at a possible worst—the entire population of the world. From one point of view it is extraordinary how few had the clarity to see this fact and the imagination to feel its horror. It is greatly to Russell's credit that he did both.

War and Peace

Russell opposed the Boer War and the First World War, supported the Allied effort in the Second World War, and laboured mightily against the imminent possibility of a Third World War and the actuality of the Vietnam War. He made war on war until his death at the age of 97. Both his early and his late anti-war activities were greeted with hostility and landed him in prison. Yet no one can now say he was wrong to take the stands he did; when the jingoism and flag-waving stops, and the awful costs are counted against a soberer assessment of the reasons why they were paid at all, people begin to see war in retrospect as Russell had the genius to see it at the time.

Russell never changed his view that the First World War was unnecessary. There was nothing really at issue between Germany and Britain in 1914 except national pride and some resolvable irritation over imperial questions. He thought that hostilities could have been avoided by negotiation, which would have soothed Germany's justifiable annoyance that it had not fared as well in the colonial race as it might have done. But the Foreign Ministries of Europe were staffed by aristocrats motivated more by considerations of *amour propre* than common sense.

Russell's opponents in the First World War argued that Germany was guilty of aggression and expansionism, and sought hegemony in Europe, which threatened Britain's liberty because, if Germany won, it would stamp its authoritarian and bureaucratic imprint over everything. Therefore Britain had an excellent motive to fight. Russell did not accept either the imputed motive or the likely outcome if Britain refused to fight; he thought it would most likely have been a rerun of the Franco-Prussian conflict of 1871, short and decisive. But even if the Kaiser won—which would be an evil, but not so great an evil as the war itself—the chief point for him was that to go to war one must have an overwhelmingly good reason to do so, and no such thing existed in 1914.

In 1939, matters were very different. During the 1930s Russell was in fact an appeaser, as his *Which Way To Peace?* of 1936 testifies. He would not let this book be reprinted, however, because by the time he finished it he had come to feel that it was insincere, and that the circumstances of the 1930s were too different from those of 1914:

I had been able to view with reluctant acquiescence the possibility of the supremacy of the Kaiser's Germany. I thought that, although this would be an evil, it would not be so great an evil as a world war and its aftermath. But Hitler's Germany was a different matter. I found the Nazis utterly revolting—cruel, bigoted, and stupid. Morally and intellectually they were alike odious to me. (*A* 430)

He found the thought of defeat by such people 'unbearable, and at last consciously and definitely decided that I must support what was necessary for victory in the Second World War, however difficult victory might be to achieve, and however painful its consequences' (ibid.).

The terrifying end to the war in the Pacific, with the dropping of atom bombs on Japanese cities, instantly alerted Russell to the fact that something quite new had entered the calculation. In a speech to the House of Lords in November 1945 he warned his peers of the dangers. At first he thought America should use its superiority in atomic weapons to coerce the Russians into not developing them. This has been interpreted as a demand by Russell that the United States should make a pre-emptive atom bomb attack on Russia; but he did not go so far. He saw that a window of opportunity existed for the United States to institute world government by means of its military superiority, and he urged it to do so. Although he thought there was a good deal wrong with America, he much preferred its generally liberal and democratic outlook to the tyranny in the Soviet Union. Indeed in the years after the Second World War Russell's hostility to the Soviet Union, already considerable as a result of his visit in the early 1920s, increased. It is a measure of his disgust at the Vietnam War just fifteen years later that he came to denounce the Americans in the same ferocious terms. The change of heart was not, however, sudden. Macarthyism in the United States, and its bellicose Macarthyite anti-communist foreign policy abroad, gradually led him to think that the Americans were a greater threat to peace than the Soviet Union. The Cuban missile crisis of 1961 confirmed him in this view. Thereafter he was determinedly anti-American.

What altered matters for Russell on the atomic weapons question was, first, Soviet acquisition of the bomb in 1949, and then, in 1954, Britain's test explosion on Bikini Atoll. In response to the latter he made a famous Christmas radio broadcast, 'Man's Peril', warning Britain and the world of the horrendous dangers to which everyone was now exposed. This broadcast was a turning point; from it dated the true beginning of campaigns against the existence of weapons of mass destruction. He was inundated with letters. Using the momentum generated by his broadcast, he organized an international petition signed by leading scientists. He never stopped demanding that Britain should scrap its nuclear weapons, one of the reasons for doing which, he argued, is to give a moral lead to other nations to do the same.

His views on how the danger now faced by the world should be managed changed during the 1950s as the international situation worsened and his own endeavours met with failure. He wrote and broadcast; in addition to his petition he organized a conference bringing together scientists from both sides of the Iron Curtain; and he participated in the setting up of the Campaign for Nuclear Disarmament (CND) and served as its first President. As these peaceful and reasoned means ran repeatedly into the brick wall of government intransigence, he became more despairing. He resigned from CND, therefore, and joined the much more militant Committee of 100, which began a campaign of civil disobedience. The campaign earned him a second prison sentence, forty-two years after the first. In all this there was little scope for theorizing, because Russell felt there was no time for it; what was needed was action.

In his very last years Russell's attention was absorbed by the Vietnam War. By now surrounded by others who made use of his name on publications and press releases which—as their grammar as well as their tone suggests—could not have emanated from him personally, he attacked the United States and, in particular, its military-industrial complex and the CIA, charging them with aggression in Vietnam and the perpetration of war crimes. With Jean-Paul Sartre and others he sponsored the International War Crimes Tribunal, aimed at putting America on trial for its activities in Vietnam. At the time people thought that the Tribunal's charges against the United States were merely hysterical. With the subsequent publication of US government files, many of the charges are now known to be true.

In at least one respect there is a remarkable consistency between Russell's opposition to the First World War and his opposition to the Vietnam War. It is that in both he thought there was no question of a genuine good at stake, and that both were prompted by the lowest instincts in man—the brutal, mindless, aggressive instincts, which, once they are in control, license anything: the bombing of women and children, the use of poison chemicals, the smokescreen of propaganda and lies directed at the home population. At the end of his very long life Russell must have found it appalling that between 1914 and 1970 weapons of war had grown more destructive than ever, but that mankind had not altered one jot.

5   Russell's Influence

If you wish to see Russell's monument, look around you at main-stream philosophy in the English language as it has been practised since the years between the two World Wars. Look also at logic, at the philosophy of mathematics, at the changed moral climate of the twentieth-century Western world, and at attempts to halt the proliferation of nuclear weapons. The complete history of any of these matters must refer to Russell.

In some of these respects he is just one actor among others; he was far from alone, for example, in bringing about the century's revolution in morals. He was much closer to centre stage in the nuclear disarmament campaign, as he had been in the pacifist movement of the First World War.

But in philosophy his place is so pivotal that, as remarked in the opening chapter, he is practically its wallpaper. His philo-sophical inheritors carry on their philosophical work in his style, addressing problems he identified or to which he gave contem-porary shape, using tools and techniques he developed, and all in large agreement with the aims and assumptions he adopted. A measure of the extraordinary pervasiveness of his influence is that many among the younger generations of twentieth-century philosophers are barely conscious that all this is owed to him.

Contemporary philosophy, said Jules Vuillemin, began with Rus-sell's *The Principles of Mathematics*. The celebrated American philosopher W. V. Quine, quoting this remark, varies the meta-phor: for him this work is 'the embryo of twentieth-century philosophy' (W. V. Quine, 'Remarks for a Memorial Symposium', in Pears, *Bertrand Russell*, 5). Quine was himself attracted to philosophy by reading Russell. As a young man his first educa-tion in logic, science, and philosophy was provided by Russell's books; like many others he felt their 'drawing power', and was lured by them first into the study of logic and the philosophy of mathematics, and then into the theory of knowledge and philo-sophy of science. 'The authentic scientific ring of Russell's logic echoed in his epistemology of natural knowledge,' Quine wrote. 'The echo was especially clear in 1914, in *Our Knowledge of the External World*. That book fired some of us, and surely Carnap for one, with new hopes for phenomenalism' (ibid. 2–3). To that book Quine adds the lectures on Logical Atomism and both *The Analysis of Mind* and *The Analysis of Matter* as seminal works: 'there is no missing [their] relevance to the Western scientific philosophy of the century' (ibid.). And there is no missing the relevance to Russell's philosophy, in turn, of his logic—'Russell's name is inseparable from mathematical logic, which owes him much'— especially the Theory of Descriptions and the Theory of Types.

Russell invented Type Theory to overcome the paradoxes he had discovered while trying to place mathematics on logical foundations (see pp. 28–39 above). During his efforts to solve this problem he canvassed a number of alternatives, including one which, ironically, was later to carry the day in set theory—in a version worked out by Ernst Zermelo—thus displacing the theory Russell eventually devised. But his theory of types was immensely influential in philosophy nevertheless. Its motivating idea was adapted by the Logical Positivists of the 1920s and 1930s in mounting their attack on metaphysics, and Gilbert Ryle applied a different version of it to the elimination of 'category mistakes', the kind of mistake exemplified by someone's thinking that the University of Oxford is an entity additional to all the colleges and institutions comprising it. In Quine's view the theory of types also influenced Edmund Husserl and, along with other aspects of Russell's logic, the great Polish logicians Stanislaw Lesniewski and Kazimierz Ajdukiewicz (Pears, *Russell*, 4).

To this must be added the importance of the Theory of Descriptions. Quine states:

Russell's logical theory of descriptions was philosophically important both for its direct bearing on philosophical issues having to do with meaning and reference, and for its illustrative value as a paradigm of philosophical analysis. Russell's theory of logical types established new trends at once in the metaphysics of ontological categories, in the antimetaphysics of logical positivism, and, overspilling philosophy at the far edge, in structural linguistics. Is it any wonder that Vuillemin sees Russell's work in logic as inaugurating contemporary philosophy'? (Pears, *Russell*, 4–5).

When Russell died Gilbert Ryle gave an obituary address to the Aristotelian Society, the chief British philosophical club, to which Russell, beginning in 1896, had often read papers. In it Ryle identified the respects in which, in his view, Russell's work had given twentieth-century philosophy 'its whole trajectory' ('Bertrand Russell: 1872–1970', reprinted in Roberts, *Bertrand Russell Memorial Volume*). One was 'a new style of philosophical work that Russell, I think virtually single-handedly, brought into the tactics of philosophical thinking' (ibid. 16). This was the use of difficult cases to test philosophical theses, a form of conceptual experimentation aimed at subjecting the claims and concepts of philosophy to scrutiny. For example, in his paper 'Mathematical Logic as based on the Theory of Types' Russell lists seven contradictions demanding solution by a competent theory, and offers it as a test of adequacy for his theory of types that it succeeds in dealing with them all. This technique is now a commonplace of philosophical method. 'Thought experiments' are devised to put a view through its paces—as in ethics, for example, where a principle is applied to a variety of increasingly difficult cases to see whether it accommodates them; or in discussions of the important forensic and metaphysical concept of personal identity, where imaginative 'survival tests' are invented to see whether we would count the persons who go into and come out of them as the 'same person'.

But even more important, in Ryle's view, is the way Russell introduced into philosophy the discipline of formal logic. 'It was due to him, as well as, to a lesser degree, to Frege and Whitehead, that some training in post-Aristotelian formal logic came fairly soon to be regarded as a *sine qua non* for the philosopher-to-be' (ibid. 19). Ryle was well placed to know; he had been instrumental in ensuring that this happened in the Oxford curriculum. And the reason for a training in logic is that it introduces rigour and promises insights of the kind exemplified in Russell's theories of descriptions and types. Like Quine, Ryle cites the latter as especially important in illustrating how sense might be distinguished from nonsense, thus, in his view, separately influencing the early Wittgenstein and the Logical Positivists.

Vuillemin nominated Russell's first major attempt to provide mathematics with logical foundations as the crucible of analytic

philosophy. This is no doubt correct, in the sense that, in preliminary and sometimes inchoate form, Russell there made his
preliminary identification of its main methods and problems. But
Quine is also right to say that it is the whole span of Russell's
works, both books and papers, between 1900 and, say, 1930, on
which analytic philosophy rests. In some of these places, however, the germs of later work are more immediately obvious. Take
for example the second chapter of *Our Knowledge of the External
World*, entitled 'Logic as the Essence of Philosophy'. This chapter
is an illustrative document in two ways. First, it is one of the
clearest statements of the aims, motivations, and methods of Russell's style of analysis. Secondly, it contains a sketch of the philosophical project which Wittgenstein adopted in his *Tractatus
Logico-Philosophicus*, showing how ideas take seed and develop.

Russell begins the second chapter of *OKEW* by asserting that
the problems of philosophy 'all reduce themselves, in so far as
they are genuinely philosophical, to problems of logic' (*OKEW*
42). By this he means that philosophical problems can be clarified
and dispelled by application of the techniques of elementary
mathematical logic, which 'enable us to deal easily with more
abstract conceptions than mere verbal reasoning can enumerate;
they suggest fruitful hypotheses which otherwise could hardly be
thought of; and they enable us to see quickly what is the smallest
store of materials with which a given logical or scientific edifice
can be constructed' (*OKEW* 51). In particular, the theories of perception and knowledge which he goes on to offer in later chapters
of *OKEW* are 'inspired by mathematical logic, and could never
have been imagined without it' (ibid.). What is chiefly in play is
the idea that logic enables us to specify the *forms* of facts and the
propositions which express them. The paradigm of an analysis
that solves a major problem by revealing the form of a proposition
is, as ever, the Theory of Descriptions. Even earlier, Russell had
employed formal analysis to show that not all propositions are
subject-predicate in form, but rather are relational; which by itself, in his view, had refuted idealism and justified the assumption of pluralism.

In discussing relations in chapter 2 of *OKEW* Russell observes
that they can only be properly understood if a classification of the
logical forms of facts is available. This is where the anticipatory

sketch of Wittgenstein's *Tractatus* occurs. The suggestion is not that Russell learned it from Wittgenstein, who during the two years before Russell wrote this chapter was his pupil in Cambridge; but rather, the other way round: Wittgenstein learned these ideas from Russell. The grounds for this claim are given shortly. First, it is necessary to remind oneself of the argument of Wittgenstein's *Tractatus*. Using Wittgenstein's own words and system of numbering rearranged (here to show the structure of the argument), the fundamental theses of the *Tractatus* are:

1. The world is all that is the case.
1.1 The world is the totality of facts, not of things.
2. What is the case—a fact—is the existence of states of affairs.
2.01 A state of affairs (a state of things) is a combination of objects (things).
2.02 Objects are simple.

Parallel to this austere description of the world's structure is a description of the corresponding structure of thought as expressed in propositions, a relation Wittgenstein calls 'picturing':

4. A logical picture of facts is a thought.
3.1 In a proposition a thought finds an expression that can be perceived by the senses.
3.201 In a proposition a thought can be expressed in such a way that the elements of the propositional sign correspond to the objects of the thought.
5. A proposition is a truth-function of elementary propositions.
4.21 The simplest kind of propositions, an elementary proposition, asserts the existence of a state of affairs.

And so on, with increasing detail. It goes without saying that the logical ideas which underlie these theses are of course familiar from earlier work by Russell; but they relate principally to the notion of structure and the means of their analysis, as exemplified in the Theory of Descriptions. Much more striking is the actual content of the views respectively expressed by Wittgenstein in the *Tractatus* and Russell in the second chapter of *OKEW*. In this chapter Russell writes:

The existing world consists of many things with many qualities and relations. A complete description of the existing world would require not only a catalogue of the things, but also a mention of all their qualities and relations. . . . When I speak of a 'fact', I do not mean one of the simple things in the world; I mean that a certain thing has a certain quality, or that certain things have a certain relation . . . Now a fact, in this sense, is never simple, but always has two or more constituents . . . Given any fact, there is a proposition which expresses the fact . . . [such a proposition] will be called an atomic proposition, because, as we shall see immediately, there are other propositions into which atomic propositions enter in a way analogous to that in which atoms enter into molecules . . . In order to preserve the parallelism in language as regards facts and propositions, we shall give the name 'atomic facts' to the facts we have hitherto been considering. [*OKEW* 60–1, 62]

And so on.

Now Russell's account here is simply a sketch, and it is inform- ally presented. In the *Tractatus* Wittgenstein sets out his theses in more detail, and in the systematically numbered format which gives it the appearance of rigour, although it is in fact only in part an argument. And Wittgenstein is careful to detach his account of the parallel world-language structures from any epistemological considerations, whereas Russell gives concrete examples of facts, qualities, and relations: an example of an atomic fact is 'this is red', of a molecular fact 'it is Monday and it is raining'.

That the basis of Wittgenstein's *Tractatus* derives from these ideas of Russell's can be shown by the fact that the sketch in Russell's chapter recapitulates a longer account he attempted to give in a manuscript now called *Theory of Knowledge* (this title was conferred on it when it was posthumously reconstructed and published). Russell was engaged on this work during 1913 while Wittgenstein was his pupil. He showed it to Wittgenstein, who criticized its discussions of acquaintance and judgement. 'Acquaintance', as described earlier, is Russell's name for funda- mental cognitive relations between a subject and objects of vari- ous kinds; 'judgement' is a complex relation roughly describable as accepting a proposition as true in virtue of acquaintance with its constituents. We do not know the details of Wittgenstein's criticisms; when Russell reported them in a letter he said: 'We were both cross from the heat. I showed him a crucial part of what I had been writing. He said it was all wrong, not realising the difficulties—that he had tried my view and knew it wouldn't work. I couldn't understand his objection—in fact he was very inarticulate—but I feel in my bones that he must be right.' Largely for this reason Russell published only part of the manuscript, and some years later gave up the concept of acquaintance which is central to it. But the basic plan—of molecular propositions analysable into atomic constituents, which express facts parallel in structure, with the relation between facts and propositions underwriting our understanding of the latter—remains in the sketch given in the second chapter of *OKEW*; and it is the skeleton upon which Wittgenstein puts somewhat different flesh in the *Tractatus*.

It is not surprising that Wittgenstein's views should derive from Russell in this way. Russell was in effect the only philosophical teacher Wittgenstein had, and, with rather few identifiable exceptions, Russell's work was his principal philosophical reading. His friend David Pinsent wrote in his diary: 'it is obvious that Wittgenstein is one of Russell's disciples and owes enormously to him.' It is clear then that one of the first philosophical offshoots from Russell's work was Wittgenstein's *Tractatus*. It can be argued that in complex and, this time, negative ways Russell is one of the chief influences on Wittgenstein's later philosophy also.

If the catalogue of Russell's influences included no more than the names already mentioned—Quine, Carnap, the Logical Positivists, Wittgenstein and Ryle; to which, by his own avowal as in the case of Quine, is to be added that of A. J. Ayer—it would be proof positive of Vuillemin's claim that Russell is the founder and presiding spirit of twentieth-century analytic philosophy. But there is much more to be said on that score; and there is also the fact that there are those who award the palm elsewhere. Both points merit discussion.

There is unhappily no index to the collection of Russell's papers edited by R. C. Marsh under the title *Logic and Knowledge*. This collection brings together some of Russell's most important and consequential essays, most of which, in turn, are required reading for analytic philosophers. They include 'The Logic of Relations', 'On Denoting', 'Mathematical Logic as Based on the Theory of Types', 'On the Nature of Acquaintance', 'The Philosophy of Logical Atomism', 'On Propositions: What they are and how they mean', and others. In the absence of an index a close student of these papers is likely to make his own pencil index on the endpapers of his copy of the book. Looking through my own I find references not only to the topics one would expect in a collection of Russell's work—descriptions, denoting, types, logical fictions, analysis, acquaintance, sense-data, relations, universals, particulars, facts, propositions, and so on—but also a list of what looks like some of analytic philosophy's special obsessions: propositional attitudes, modality and possible worlds, vagueness, naturalism, truth-functionality, the nature of mind, verification, truth, existence, meaning, and much more. A very great deal of this comes from Russell himself, and in focus and range his work therefore constitutes a marked change of direction in the history of philosophy. Even the five contemporaries Russell most frequently cites in acknowledgements—and he was extraordinarily generous, indeed overgenerous, in attributing the source of his inspirations to others—namely, Peano, Frege, Whitehead, Moore, and William James, only one is comparable in discussing this kind and (to a lesser degree) range of topics, and that is Frege.

But although Frege influenced Russell, and did brilliant work in the philosophy of mathematics and language, his influence on Russell was less than one might suppose: for Russell did not understand Frege when he first read him, and had to rediscover some of Frege's views for himself before he grasped their significance; and even then, on certain crucial points such as Frege's distinction between sense and reference, he did not take Frege's point and drew a different and less happy distinction of his own. Moreover Frege's focus, though deeper, was narrower than Russell's, so Russell's application of the new ideas in mathematical logic to wider concerns of philosophy was effectively without precedent. The originality of Russell's contributions is therefore great.

Russell's influence worked in other ways too. In the third chapter of *OKEW* he approached the problem of accounting for spatial perception by constructing a 'model hypothesis' as a possible explanation of how the highly perspectival private spaces experienced by individuals in vision and touch, come to be commensurate with the private spaces of others in public space. He did this by setting up a model and then 'paring away what is superfluous in our hypothesis, leaving a residue which may be regarded as the abstract answer to our problem' (*OKEW* 94). He takes us step by step through a construction showing how to overcome an important apparent discrepancy between the world of sense and the world of physics. A similar technique was adopted later by

P. F. Strawson in his book *Individuals*, where he used it in constructing a purely auditory world to explore the concepts of basic particulars and reidentification. And it was used by A. J. Ayer in his *Central Questions of Philosophy* to determine how much in the way of perceptual and conceptual capacities we must grant a perceiver as a basis for his having perceptual experience. There are other examples besides.

One striking feature of Russell's legacy is that it is almost wholly philosophical rather than logical or mathematical. This fact requires explanation. G. T. Kneebone remarked: 'For all the inspiration that *Principia Mathematica* has communicated to the logicians and philosophers of the twentieth century, and for all its rich fecundity as a source of concepts and symbolic devices, this great work remains, in the literature of the foundations of mathematics, a lone classic without progeny.' This assessment is not strictly true; the felicities of logical notation introduced by *Principia* form the basis of what is now standard, and there have been versions of some of *Principia*'s technicalities, for example Quine's version of type theory. But it is broadly true, and this is what invites comment. Briefly, what might be said is this: during and after the period in which *Principia* was written there was an explosion in mathematical and logical research, which it is fair to say quickly rendered *Principia* obsolete. A variety of logics was formulated, logic-free formalizations of arithmetic were discovered, logic and set-theory both turned out to be relative (that is, developments in various approaches showed that there is no unique or 'absolute' logic or set theory), Zermelo-Fraenkel set theory displaced type-theoretic set theory, and Kurt Gödel's incompleteness theorem, which in essence states that neither mathematics nor logic can be axiomatized, blocks Russell's logicist hope of explaining the source and justification of mathematical knowledge in logical terms.

Accordingly, the project of *Principia*, and Russell's attempts to overcome the technical difficulties in the way of carrying it out, are valuable chiefly because of their 'spin-offs' for philosophy rather than for their place in the history of mathematics. The same is true of the work of Frege, except that some of his technical innovations in the formalities of logic were immensely important for its subsequent development.

Frege is the other great thinker at the beginning of the twentieth century who is credited with founding analytic philosophy. The scholar who puts Frege at the centre of the century's philosophical map, Michael Dummett, argues that the essence of analytic philosophy is the claim that in order to understand how we think about the world, we must examine language, because language is our only route to thought. This makes the philosophy of language central, displacing the theory of knowledge which, since at least Descartes's time, had held this position. And this displacement of theory of knowledge by philosophy of language owes itself, says Dummett, to Frege. Frege had embarked on the same programme as Russell—beginning two decades earlier—of basing mathematics on logic. He found the logical tools available to him hopelessly inadequate for the task. So he set about inventing new ones; and succeeded. His innovations both simplified logic and greatly extended its power. But he also saw that he would have to examine notions of reference, truth, and meaning to carry out his project, and this, says Dummett, is where a turn to the philosophy of language began.

Without question Frege's work is of the first importance in philosophy. It is also without question that Frege influenced Russell, although in the equivocal way sketched a few paragraphs above. But it is hard to agree with Dummett's claim of historical priority for Frege—and not just because Dummett's conception of analytic philosophy is unrealistically restrictive. The fact is that Frege's work was very little known during his own lifetime (he died in 1925), and Russell was almost alone in trying to bring it to wider notice. Even then, it was not until the 1950s—and really not until the first of Dummett's major studies of Frege in the 1960s—that the full import of his work was appreciated. On the purely historical question it would be more correct to say that the outstanding value of Frege's ideas is a function of their theoretical rather than their historical importance. For quite a lot of Russell's work —his theories of perception and knowledge, his philosophies of mind and science—it would be fair to say that the reverse is true: their importance is historical rather than theoretical. But some of Russell's work, as we have seen, combines both theoretical and historical value, and that is why it is seminal for analytic philosophy.

The claims of G. E. Moore to a founding role in analytic philosophy are also sometimes advanced, and not without cause. Russell, in his generous way, attributed his emergence from idealism to the influence of Moore, and there is no doubt that Moore's philosophical temperament and methods had an effect on him. Moore claimed that whereas most philosophers began to philosophize because of wonder, his reason for doing so was that he found what other philosophers said astonishing. His technique was to search for definitions of the key terms or concepts under discussion in some area of philosophical enquiry. He required of definition that the definiens (the statement of definition) should be synonymous with the definiendum (the expression or concept being defined) but contain no terms in common with it. The trouble with this is that even if such definitions were possible—and there is doubt that they are, even in the case of lexical definitions such as are commonplace in dictionaries—they constitute only one kind of definition, and the other kinds, for example analytic definitions (defining something by describing its structure or function) and definitions in use (allowing something to explain itself by showing it at work), are often not only more practical but more revealing; and therefore philosophically more valuable. Moore of course recognized the existence and utility of other kinds of definitions, but regarded his preferred kind as the ideal; and he also held that in the case of certain fundamental philosophical notions, such as that of 'goodness' in ethics, no definition is possible: such things are indefinable and primitive, and theory must begin with them rather than attempt to explain them.

Again without doubt, Moore's style and personality were important in the early years of analytic philosophy. In the introduction to *OKEW* Russell wrote that analysis introduced into philosophy what Galileo had introduced into physics: 'the substitution of piecemeal, detailed and verifiable results for large untested generalities recommended only by a certain appeal to the imagination'. This could equally well serve as a characterization of Moore's painstaking style of philosophy, in which he takes a claim or idea and worries away at it endlessly until it is in its component pieces, neatly laid out. It is not a dashing style, but it is effective in its limited way. Moore had quite a number of imitators, but his aims and methods were chiefly critical; he did not make any philosophical discoveries. His main legacy is that he gave currency to the notion of a 'naturalistic fallacy' in ethics, which is to define the moral property of goodness in terms of some natural property like pleasure. The measure of a philosopher's influence is the use made of his methods and ideas after he introduced them; by this measure Moore's place at the beginning of twentieth-century philosophy does not compare with Russell's. He did, however, help to set the analytical mood, and his famous mannerism—the shocked intake of breath with which he greeted philosophical remarks that seemed to him bizarre—helped to make generations of pupils and colleagues think much more carefully before they spoke or wrote.

In the foregoing discussion the implication might seem to be that analytic philosophy is a recent phenomenon. In the sense that many of its contemporary inspirations and techniques are drawn from the fundamentals of the new logic, this is true; but in another and equally important sense it represents a direct development of the tradition of Hume, Berkeley, Locke, and Aristotle. The first two of these thinkers—and especially the second—together with Leibniz provided Russell with much of his philosophical outlook. It is not difficult to see the similarity between Russell and Aristotle, for the latter based his metaphysics on his logic, and developed his logic for the purpose, just as Russell did.

No assessment of Russell as a philosopher can ignore the fact that, too often, his work is much less rigorous and careful than it would have been had he observed his own methodological counsels. There are indeed some notorious stretches of carelessness and superficiality in his work, and it is a standing wonder in the philosophical profession that his most successful and widely read book, *A History of Western Philosophy*, arguably the source of most people's knowledge of philosophy, is—despite its many other virtues—in a number of places woefully inadequate as philosophical discussion. He made mistakes which students are now on their guard against in their earliest essays; for example, the 'use-mention' distinction, which marks the large difference between actually using an expression and talking about it. In the preceding sentence I used the word 'expression'; I am now mentioning it, marking the fact by enclosing it in quotation marks. There are many occasions in philosophical debate where the distinction is crucial, a point that can be simply made by noting that very different things are meant by 'Cicero has six letters' and ' "Cicero" has six letters'.

Russell's occasional insouciance about the need to be finicky (an inescapable duty in philosophy, if one is to be exact, clear, and rigorous: philosophy also requires imagination and creativity, but unless imagination is combined with precision it gets no one far) has irritated some. Reviewing *Human Knowledge*, Norman Malcolm described it as 'the patter of a conjurer'. Paradoxically, Russell raised standards a long way in philosophical debate, but by the exigent levels those standards have reached, he is himself now sometimes found wanting.

These complaints are, however, minor. In most cases where Russell sails rapidly past qualifications and minutiae in his marvellous prose, beguiling us with his wit, such problems as he causes are not very great if the reader is alert. In any case Russell was aware of the fact that he sometimes went too fast. He was impatient with the kind of pedantry that is happy only when up to its neck in footnotes. He was anxious for practical results, for a working, stable view of the best grounding in experience that science can have. In some of his later work especially, his attitude was that if the larger outlines of a theory were plotted, its details could be filled in later. Even then his ideas are stimulating and sometimes novel.

But these remarks, one notes, apply only to Russell in a hurry, working in charcoal rather than oils. At his best his philosophical work is rich, detailed, ingenious, and profound. This is particularly true of what he wrote in the period between 1900 and 1914. The papers collected in *Logic and Knowledge* speak for themselves in this respect. What R. L. Goodstein says of some of the work in *Principia*—'In certain respects the *Principia* represents a peak of intellectual attainment; in particular the ramified theory of types with the axiom of reducibility is as subtle and ingenious a concept as is to be found anywhere in the whole literature of logic and mathematics' ('Post *Principia*', in Roberts, *Russell Memorial Volume*, 128)—can be applied to some of Russell's more important philosophical writings. This is high praise indeed.

The graph of reputation has an almost invariable curve. It rises during life, and even if it dips in the fading years it makes a jump at the time of obituaries and memorials. Then it plunges and lies flat for a generation. But at length it rises again and finds its proper level in the estimation of posterity. Russell died in 1970; in the decades since then his name—but not, as much in the foregoing pages shows, his real influence—has been present only in particular connection with those topics in philosophy where his work is central: chiefly in discussion of reference and descriptions, in analyses of existence, and in the recent history of the theory of perception. One reason for this sidelining into footnotes is that for a time the later philosophy of Wittgenstein (who bucks the trend of the graph; immediately after his death there were three decades of enthusiastic discipleship, but his gifts as a philosopher—great though they are—are now more soberly appreciated) opposed something quite different to the Russellian style of analysis. In fact, most people working in philosophy continued in Russell's style, but the celebrity of Wittgensteinian ideas and the energy of his disciples almost gave the contrary impression. The key here is Ryle's remark that Russell did not seek or desire to found a school of disciples: 'Russell taught us not to think his thoughts but how to move in our own philosophical thinking. In one way no one is now or will ever again be a Russellian; but in another way every one of us is now something of a Russellian.'

Generally speaking, thinkers accumulate disciples when they offer attractive-sounding answers to the great questions of philosophy (which, in more popular garb, are the great questions of life). Russell was sceptical about answers, although he vigorously sought them. In the conclusion of *The Problems of Philosophy*, speaking of the value of philosophy, he wrote:

Philosophy is to be studied, not for the sake of any definite answers to its questions, since no definite answers can, as a rule, be known to be true, but rather for the sake of the questions themselves; because these questions enlarge our conception of what is possible, enrich our intellectual imagination, and diminish the dogmatic assurance which closes the mind against speculation; but above all because, through the greatness of the universe which philosophy contemplates, the mind also is rendered great, and becomes capable of that union with the universe which constitutes the highest good.

By whichever measure one chooses, Russell, who contemplated many universes, is a great mind. He changed the course of philosophy and gave it a new character. There are very few figures in history of whom, with respect to their own sphere of activity, this can be said. And even then, some of these achieved it by accident or one momentary endeavour, as did—for good and ill respectively—Alexander Fleming and Gavrilo Princip. Russell, in contrast, achieved it by monumental means: in many books, articles, and lectures, over many years, across many continents. In the company of such as Aristotle, Newton, Darwin, and Einstein he is, therefore, a truly epic figure.

Further Reading

RUSSELL's works remain their own best introduction, but there is a large literature on Russell and the various aspects of his philosophy, some of which carries much further the debates he started. A. J. Ayer's *Bertrand Russell* (London: Fontana, 1972) and *Russell and Moore: The Analytical Heritage* (Cambridge, Mass.: Harvard University Press, 1971) provide a sympathetic introduction. R. M. Sainsbury's *Russell* (London: Routledge, 1979) gives an absorbing technical discussion of Russell's central work. Peter Hylton's *Russell, Idealism and the Emergence of Analytic Philosophy* (Oxford: Clarendon Press, 1990) is essential reading for any serious study of Russell's thought. Nicholas Griffin's *Russell's Idealist Apprenticeship* (Oxford: Clarendon Press, 1991) is an excellent detailed study of Russell's early work in philosophy.

There are a number of collections of essays on aspects of Russell's work. E. D. Klemke (ed.), *Essays on Bertrand Russell* (Urbana: University of Illinois Press, 1971), D. F. Pears (ed.), *Bertrand Russell* (New York: Anchor Books, 1972), G. W. Roberts (ed.), *Bertrand Russell Memorial Volume* (London: Allen & Unwin, 1979), P. A. Schilpp (ed.), *The Philosophy of Bertrand Russell* (New York: Tudor Publishing, 3rd edn., 1951; with Russell's replies to the essays), are to be found in most academic libraries and between them cover much ground.

Alan Ryan's *Bertrand Russell: A Political Life* (London: Penguin Books, 1988) is excellent on the 'applied' side of Russell's activities.

Other works cited in the main text are: Michael Dummett, *Frege: Philosophy of Language*, 2nd edn. (London: Duckworth, 1981); A. J. Ayer, *Central Questions of Philosophy* (London: Weidenfeld & Nicolson, 1973); William James, *Essays in Radical Empiricism* (New York: Longmans, 1912); P. F. Strawson, 'On Referring', *Mind* (1950), reprinted in Strawson, *Logico-Linguistic Papers* (London: Methuen, 1971), and *Individuals* (London: Methuen, 1959); and F. H. Bradley, *Appearance and Reality* (Oxford: Oxford University Press, 1897).

Index

Index

OXFORD

MORE OXFORD PAPERBACKS

This book is just one of nearly 1000 Oxford Paperbacks currently in print. If you would like details of other Oxford Paperbacks, including titles in the World's Classics, Oxford Reference, Oxford Books, OPUS, Past Masters, Oxford Authors, and Oxford Shakespeare series, please write to:

UK and Europe: Oxford Paperbacks Publicity Manager, Arts and Reference Publicity Department, Oxford University Press, Walton Street, Oxford OX2 6DP.

Customers in UK and Europe will find Oxford Paperbacks available in all good bookshops. But in case of difficulty please send orders to the Cash-with-Order Department, Oxford University Press Distribution Services, Saxon Way West, Corby, Northants NN18 9ES. Tel: 01536 741519; Fax: 01536 746337. Please send a cheque for the total cost of the books, plus £1.75 postage and packing for orders under £20; £2.75 for orders over £20. Customers outside the UK should add 10% of the cost of the books for postage and packing.

USA: Oxford Paperbacks Marketing Manager, Oxford University Press, Inc., 200 Madison Avenue, New York, N.Y. 10016.

Canada: Trade Department, Oxford University Press, 70 Wynford Drive, Don Mills, Ontario M3C 1J9.

Australia: Trade Marketing Manager, Oxford University Press, G.P.O. Box 2784Y, Melbourne 3001, Victoria.

South Africa: Oxford University Press, P.O. Box 1141, Cape Town 8000.

PAST MASTERS

A wide range of unique, short, clear introductions to the lives and work of the world's most influential thinkers. Written by experts, they cover the history of ideas from Aristotle to Wittgenstein. Readers need no previous knowledge of the subject, so they are ideal for students and general readers alike.

Each book takes as its main focus the thought and work of its subject. There is a short section on the life and a final chapter on the legacy and influence of the thinker. A section of further reading helps in further research.

The series continues to grow, and future Past Masters will include **Owen Gingerich** on *Copernicus*, **R G Frey** on *Joseph Butler*, **Bhiku Parekh** on *Gandhi*, **Christopher Taylor** on *Socrates*, **Michael Inwood** on *Heidegger*, and **Peter Ghosh** on *Weber*.